Lane provides practical tools to hel
sages. Anyone who preaches or tea
—*Mark Batterson, New York Time.
Lead Pastor, Nationa*

Preaching is one of the most fierce, daunting and rewarding tasks a pastor will ever undertake. You need every resource you can get to help you get better. Lane has written a cogent, helpful book that can only help you get better.

—*Carey Nieuwhof, author of Lasting Impact,
Founding Pastor, Connexus Church, Barrie, Ontario*

Lane has written a very helpful, practical book for preachers and teachers. I think there are two great sins in preaching: misusing the text and boring your audience. In teaching pastors and seminary students, I find there are plenty of resources and attention given to avoid the first great sin. But there is a lack of resources on how not to bore people. And too many preachers feel that if they have rightly divided the Word of Truth, they have done everything God requires them to do. I think accuracy and effectiveness are equally important in preaching. *Preaching Killer Sermons* is a great resource to help pastors truly be effective in communicating the powerful truth of God's Word. I plan to start using this with the preaching students I teach.

—*David Whiting, Executive Search Consultant, Vanderbloemen Group,
former Lead Pastor, Northridge Church, Rochester, NY*

Preaching Killer Sermons is a book that should be on every preacher's bookshelf: Senior Pastors, Youth Pastors, Evangelists, and even Seminary students. In his usual style, Lane gives preachers a resource that is insanely practical and challenging all at the same time. If you read this book, you will improve as a preacher/speaker…period. Whether you've been preaching for decades or only a few weeks, this book is for YOU.

—*Tim Parsons, leadership blogger, TimParsons.me
Executive Pastor, First Assembly Community Ministries*

The hardest thing I do each week is not leadership development or pastoral care - it's crafting a message which will communicate truth in an engaging and impactful way. I genuinely want to get better at what I believe is God's greatest call on my life. I'm thankful for Lane's heart to help us be better preachers. I'm thankful for this book.
 —*Ron Edmondson, Senior Pastor, Immanuel Baptist Church, Lexington, KY*
 Church leadership blogger, RonEdmondson.com

Pastor Lane Sebring has done an outstanding job of reverse engineering the "great sermon." His efforts will help all who preach to preach better prepared sermons, and become better prepared communicators. *Preaching Killer Sermons* should be included reading in homiletics courses around the world.
 —*Brett Fuller, Senior Pastor, Grace Covenant Church, Chantilly, VA*
 Chaplain, Washington Redskins

If you are a communicator in the local church you need to pick up this book. Lane brings practical insights and helpful encouragement on every page. Pick it up ... and apply the lessons contained within.
 —*Rich Birch, unSeminary*
 Executive Pastor, Liquid Church, Mountainside NJ

Preaching Killler Sermons will not only save you time and spare you stress in your sermon preparation, but will help you deliver a message that really makes a difference in people's lives. Whether you preach once a week or once a year, you will find this book incredibly practical and helpful. I wish I had this years ago!
 —*Tim Coressel, Youth & Community Life Pastor,*
 Cross Current Church, Ashburn, VA

Lane wrote *Preaching Killer Sermons* based on 10 years of ministry experience. While it is reasonable to assume that a young man such as he can share helpful insights with men just starting out in ministry, does he have anything to add to the knowledge and skill set of men who have decades of ministry experience? Yes!! I have had the privilege of being the Senior Pastor of the church at which Lane has served for

the past 9 years. Although I've been in ministry for over 3 decades, I have personally benefited from Lane's insight, convictions and suggestions. The concepts he shares in this book have helped sharpen my effectiveness in communicating the content of God's inerrant Word! I would highly recommend this book to both the novice and the experienced preacher.
> –*Dr. Billy Ross, Senior Pastor, Centreville Baptist Church, Centreville, VA*
> *Trustee, The Southern Baptist Theological Seminary*

I serve on a Teaching Team with Lane, so I watch him live out *Preaching Killer Sermons* each week. Lane's heart is to communicate God's Word in culturally relevant and engaging ways. Now he's sharing his passion in a book full of practical tools to help preachers (and teachers/speakers). Lane writes like he preaches, as if he's having a conversation with a good friend about his favorite topic. You'll hear his heart as he challenges you to examine and refine your own preaching habits.
> –*Elaine Bonds, MA in Biblical Studies, Dallas Theological Seminary,*
> *anticipated completion August 2016, sought after speaker,*
> *Graduate, Proverbs 31 She Speaks and CLASSeminars*

PREACHING KILLER SERMONS

**How to Create & Deliver
Messages that Captivate & Inspire**

LANE SEBRING

PREACHING KILLER SERMONS

Published by Preaching Donkey
Centreville, VA 20121

All rights reserved. No part of this publication may be reproduced, distributed, or transmitted in any form or by any means, including photocopying, recording, or other electronic or mechanical methods, without the prior written permission of the publisher, except in the case of brief quotations embodied in critical reviews and certain other noncommercial uses permitted by copyright law.

Any Internet addresses (websites, blogs, etc.), telephone numbers, authors and thought-leaders referenced in this book are offered as a resource to the reader. They are not intended in any way to be or imply an endorsement on the part of the author or publisher, nor do they vouch for their content.

Scripture quotations are from the ESV® Bible (*The Holy Bible, English Standard Version*®), copyright © 2001 by Crossway, a publishing ministry of Good News Publishers. Used by permission. All rights reserved. *Italics* in Scripture quotations are the author's emphasis.

Names and events in this book are the product of the author's imagination, based on his years of experience preaching and leading in local church settings and helping others do the same. Any resemblance to any person, living or dead, is coincidental.

Copyright © 2016 Lane Sebring

ISBN-13: 978-1505911336
ISBN-10: 1505911338

Printed in the United States of America
First Edition 2016

To the amazing readers of PreachingDonkey.com who continually strive to be the best preachers you can be.

CONTENTS

Introduction: Every Preacher's Biggest Challenge   1

PART ONE: COMMUNICATION KILLERS

1   The Anatomy of a Boring Sermon   17
How to Ensure No One Pays Attention

PART TWO: KILLER PREPARATION

2   Teamwork Makes the Dream Work   29
A Liberating Approach to Collaborative Preparation

3   Finding Time to Prepare   41
How to Take Control of Your Weekly Schedule

4   Every Sermon Needs a Job   55
Put Your Sermon to Work

5   Building Blocks   69
Outlines, Illustrations, and Application

6   Who Do You Think You're Talking To?   93
Know Your Listeners Inside and Out

7   The Holy Spirit and Sermon Prep   101
How God Speaks to You in Your Prep

PART THREE: KILLER DELIVERY

8 Give Them a Reason to Keep Listening 109
Why Your Listeners Must Feel it Before They Care about It

9 The Balancing Act That Makes or Breaks Delivery 119
Find Your Rhythm Between Intensity and Relief

10 Be Totally Present When You Preach 139
Overcome Distractions, Preach Boldly

11 Deliver the Goods 153
Get to the Point, Nail the Ending

PART FOUR: KILLING YOURSELF

12 The #1 Thing Most Preachers Neglect 173
How to Take Care of Yourself

Conclusion: Preach with Godfidence 185

References 190

ACKNOWLEDGEMENTS

I want to thank my amazing wife, Rachel, for supporting me and believing in me every step of the way. Without you, this would not have come to fruition.

Orval and Elaine Bonds for believing in me, investing in this project and backing it financially. Your support means more to me than you know.

My pastor, Dr. Billy Ross, for challenging me to take my preaching and leadership to the next level. Thanks for investing in me through these years of ministry together.

The people at CBC–you are like family. Your love for my family and me makes ministering with you a joy.

The Preaching Donkey community–thank you for your dedication to become better communicators of the gospel of Christ. It is a joy to learn and grow with you.

My editor, Scott Philip Stewart, you do great work.

My amazing friends and family who supported me this whole way. Your encouragement means so much.

Finally, my God who loves me and called me into his ministry. Thank you for allowing me to do what I love.

INTRODUCTION

Every Preacher's Biggest Challenge

I shuffled my notes and closed my Bible as the worship leader tuned his guitar and the musicians quietly made their way onto the stage. Rubbing my sweaty palm on my jeans, I began praying aloud to close the sermon. "Father, speak to us as we reflect on the truth we've just heard from your Word…" My mind wandered. *Did I say everything I needed to say? Did I get in everything that I had meticulously prepared?* I asked myself these questions as I muttered through the closing prayer.

If you're like me, you've probably finished preaching a sermon and asked yourself similar questions. But do those questions matter if no one was listening? What difference does it make whether you said what you planned to say if few people truly heard it? As preachers tasked with communicating the truths of Scripture to an increasingly distracted audience, we should ask ourselves a better question: *Was anyone actually listening so they could do something with it?*

A sermon can only be effective if people hear it. In his letter to the Romans, Paul hinged the effectiveness of spreading the gospel on whether people hear the message: *So faith comes from hearing, and hearing through the word of Christ (Romans 10:17).* This is true in an ultimate sense because people need to hear the gospel to respond to it and surrender their lives to Jesus. But this is also true in a practical, week-to-week preaching context: before people can benefit from what you are saying, they have to *listen* to what you are saying.

What we preachers need from our listeners is one of the most difficult things to get and one of the most challenging things to keep once you have it: *their attention.* When someone gives us their attention it is a gift. We should never take it for granted because we can lose it much easier than we gain it.

One of the most devastating mistakes we can make is to assume that if we are preaching, people are listening. Just because we stand in the front of the room with a Bible in hand does not mean people are giving us their ear. But if they don't, we will not be effective.

Since people are not going to listen to us just because we are saying words into a microphone, it is our responsibility to capture and maintain their interest. This is more challenging than you might think.

ATTENTION IS HARD TO COME BY

It is more important than ever to work on gaining and keeping the attention of our listeners when we preach. This is one of the more difficult tasks for a communicator. Despite popular opinion, the challenge is not *merely* a result of diminished attention spans. While attention spans may be shorter than a generation ago, they don't tell the whole story. I do believe shorter sermons are almost always better (more on that in chapter 11), but what makes them better has more to do with how preparing a shorter sermon forces you to deliver a tighter sermon because you have no time to waste on filler content and rambling. The sermon has a sharper focus and a higher impact.

We have to work harder to gain and keep our listeners' attention because multiple distractions compete for it every time we preach. Some of these distractions are new, and some are as timeless as humanity, but they are all present every time we stand up to deliver a message. Here are four examples:

All of the world's information is held in their hands, and it is not their Bibles. Every time you preach, almost everyone is sitting there with a smartphone in hand. They can access anything they want right in the moment. From scanning their Facebook newsfeed, to playing a mindless game, to texting a friend, to sending an email, to checking the score of the game—your listeners have everything they need to pay zero attention to your sermon.

You have three choices, and only one of them is a good one. First, you could demand that everyone check their cell phones at the door. Good luck with that. Second, you could give up and assume that no one is going to pay attention because *how can you compete with their phones?*

Or third, you can decide to give people a better reason to listen to you. This is the best and only option for those who desire to preach killer sermons. Decide to do everything you can to bring your best efforts—your 'A' game—every time and make your listeners want to put down their phones because they don't want to miss out. You can make it your goal to have only two things happening on your listeners' phones: (1) they are accessing the biblical text you are preaching on and (2) they are taking notes. This is a goal you can reach! But of course this is not the only obstacle competing for your listeners' attention.

They may think your message is irrelevant to their lives. A challenge every preacher faces is that some in our churches perceive our message as utterly irrelevant to their lives.

They are not hostile about it, and they would never say such a thing (well, most wouldn't). But it is written all over their faces. Their lives attest to it because they remain unchanged.

As a preacher who wants to communicate well, you have to engage this type of person. You begin with a deficit in their mind, and it is up to you to do something about it, find a way to make a deposit, and get in the black.

There is no magic bullet to solve this problem because people tune us out as irrelevant for various reasons. But, we do need to preach with this in mind. It takes a unique approach to attract and keep the attention of those who see the Bible, God, church, worship, fellowship, and you as altogether unremarkable and inconsequential to their daily lives. So what can you do about perceived irrelevance? This book will help you with that.

Their default is boredom. You absolutely must be interesting. If you truly believe that what you have to say has the potential to change lives, then it matters to you if they are bored. If they are checked out and just going through the motions, you must take note of this and up your game.

The difference between effective communication and mediocre preaching is how the preacher engages the mind, will, and emotions of the listener. The Killer Delivery section will reveal practical ways to ensure you're connecting with your listeners on these three levels. But, there is one more obstacle competing for your listeners' attention.

They may not accept the Bible as true and don't care whether you say it is God's Word. This last category is just good old-fashioned skepticism. Some people in your audience—probably more than you think—simply do not believe. Any number of things may be running through their minds as you preach:

- They do not believe in God.
- They believe in God but do not believe he is active in the world.
- They believe God is active in the world but do not believe the Bible is God's Word.
- They believe the Bible is God's Word ... but may not believe it is all true.
- They believe what they want to believe and have decided that nothing you say is going to change that.

Just because you have the title "Pastor" and speak from the Bible does not mean your listeners automatically give you their trust and confidence. It may in fact mean just the opposite. The point is: it is your job to earn the trust and confidence of your listeners. Ultimately, we need to be aware of these challenges so we can pray and prepare accordingly. It is more important than ever that we are mindful of unbelief and equipped to do everything we can to disarm skepticism and connect with people.

This book will equip you to engage the hearts of all your listeners—believers, unbelievers, skeptics, and the faithful alike—in the most effective way possible.

Every week you face these four competing distractions: people have the world in their hands, they may not think your message is relevant, they may be bored, and they may or may not believe that what you are saying is true. What do you do about this?

Although these obstacles are largely out of your control, this book will focus on two things you do have control over: you and your message. The following chapters will equip you with an effective way to prepare and deliver sermons for maximum impact. You will also discover the importance of taking care of yourself not only to achieve maximum output but to ensure that you last for the long haul.

YOU CAN BECOME A KILLER COMMUNICATOR

The good news is that you have a choice. You can make a decision to become a killer communicator, and this book will get you started on your journey. In my own preaching, I see only two options: either I will continually strive to become a more effective communicator, or I will lose the attention of my listeners and slip into the abyss of irrelevance. I don't want to be ineffective any more than you do. All of us want to be used to our maximum capacity, and I am thrilled that you have decided to begin this journey.

Note that this is not just about crafting great sermons; it is about developing yourself into a great communicator. Most preaching books focus on content—*what* you preach; this one is all about communication—*how* you preach. Preaching is a unique art, and much has been written about how to do it correctly. This book goes beyond what makes a sermon "textbook correct" to what makes a sermon *work*.

What works in preaching? What doesn't work? This book gets to the nitty gritty of preparing yourself, preparing your sermon, and delivering your message in a compelling way.

WHAT YOU WILL GET OUT OF THIS BOOK

This book is divided into four parts. Part 1 begins by fleshing out the problem: that communication, though important, is not easy. Parts 2 and 3 will explore effective ways to prepare and deliver sermons. Finally, part 4 will explore the importance of taking care of yourself.

Part 1: Communication Killers. Speaking is easy; communication is not. In this section we will examine the challenges most pastors face when they want to move past simply giving sermons and truly begin connecting with their audiences. This section of the book will help if the frustration most pastors feel when they ask the tough question "Is anyone paying attention?" resonates with you.

Part 2: Killer Preparation. This section focuses on preparing the sermon. The sermon is its own animal and you must tame it with a dedicated focus. Where do you begin? How do you establish effective sermon preparation practices?

You will discover some best practices for sermon preparation, such as understanding the importance of *team* preparation, setting a preparation schedule, deciding on an objective and desired response for every sermon, and more.

Part 3: Killer Delivery. This section focuses on sermon delivery and answers such questions as: What are the essential elements of killer sermon delivery? How do you communicate in such a way that people pay attention and want to hear more?

Discover how to preach conversationally as though you are talking with each person in the room, how to get to the point and make it powerfully, how to make every word count, how to nail the ending of your sermon, and much more.

Part 4: Killing Yourself. In this section the focus is you. You can prepare a great sermon, but if you are not bringing your best efforts you will suffer. As a communicator, you need to be on top of your game every time.

If you want to stay in ministry for the long haul, you cannot neglect your health and vitality as a leader. This section focuses on how you can take care of yourself so you can be an effective leader and preacher.

BEFORE YOU READ

This book deals primarily with effective communication and what it takes to prepare and deliver killer sermons. If you are looking for a standard volume on how to preach textbook sermons, you have the wrong book. But if you are truly interested in how to take your preaching to the next level by communicating more clearly every time you preach, this book is for you.

This book is not meant to encompass everything related to preaching, so I am making some assumptions about you. These assumptions allow me to focus exclusively on communication because I am assuming that some other important bases are already covered. Here's what I believe about you:

- You pray, especially when you prepare sermons.
- You believe the gospel changes lives.
- You believe the Word of God is primary in preaching.
- You believe preaching matters.
- You believe preaching works.

- You believe God can use you.
- You want God to use you.
- You know the only way for preaching to truly be effective is through God's power.
- You are perfectly comfortable with the fact that God changes lives, but you still work like crazy to improve your craft and be the best possible steward of your calling.

If the above statements are true about you, then you will find this book to be a useful tool to help you achieve your highest potential as a preacher. Remember that these themes are implied throughout the book, even though they are not reiterated in every chapter. Yes, keep praying before, during, and after each sermon. Yes, let God be the one to change hearts. Yes, preach the Word and not your own opinions. But let's also discover how to equip ourselves as the best possible vessels for God to do his amazing, life-changing work through us.

Finally, although this material will be helpful no matter your context, it is primarily for pastors who preach in a local church setting. For the sake of consistency through the chapters I have kept the focus intentionally narrow on church preaching. The principles, however, can apply easily in almost any setting where you are seeking to present content in a compelling way.

WHERE I AM COMING FROM

I used to joke with a friend about what it would be like to write a book on humility. We would try to think of possible titles: *Be Humble, Just Like Me* or *How I Mastered Perfect Humility*. Obviously, you would have to be incredibly arrogant to write a book on humility by claiming that you'd mastered it. You would open yourself up to lots of (well-deserved) criticism. It would be absurd to claim you had mastered humility because as soon as you think you are completely humble you've only proven that you're not.

I assure you that preaching is not something I have mastered. I do not claim to have it perfected or all figured out. Those who think they have mastered preaching don't really get it. Preaching is something that requires a lifetime of improvement and development. This book highlights what I have discovered in my 10 years of preaching. It also highlights what I am continuing to discover and put into practice. I do not claim to know everything about preaching. I have a lot to learn and improve on. I simply want to share my experience and help as many preachers as I can.

While completing my seminary degree in pastoral ministry, I noticed that my preaching courses focused mostly on theological accuracy, biblical exegesis, and sermon structure. Although these are all necessary, communicating effectively is too important to be ignored. If no one is listening to your message, then it does not matter how theologically accurate, biblically sound, or well-organized your sermons are.

My aim is to take you on a journey toward preaching with greater impact. I draw from my decade of practical experience in preaching, my degree in communications, and my master's in pastoral ministry. But more than anything I draw from my love for preaching and my obsession with listening to preaching. I have been inspired by those preachers who are able to make my spirit come alive. There is something so fascinating to me about captivating preaching. I have also been uninspired by preaching so unremarkable it makes me angry that someone would abuse the craft by making a sermon boring (Though, I admit I've been guilty of this at times).

I have studied, analyzed, and thought deeply about what makes some preaching amazing and life-changing and other preaching just "meh." I want to help preachers with the insights I have gained and lessons learned through my own trial and error. This book is a result of a decade-long journey to discover and now articulate what makes preaching effective and life-changing.

One of my greatest passions in life is preaching, and I look forward to improving together. Let's get started!

LANE SEBRING

PART ONE

COMMUNICATION KILLERS

LANE SEBRING

CHAPTER ONE

The Anatomy of a Boring Sermon
How to Ensure No One Pays Attention

Ryan had been the senior pastor at Community Church for six years. He had to chuckle when the elders insisted on his title because he was the only person on staff. Nonetheless, Ryan was the "senior" pastor. He was also the receptionist, administrative assistant, worship service planner, counselor, accountant, bookkeeper, and ... oh yeah ... he also preached 50 weeks a year because, after all, he was the senior pastor. That's what they paid him to do, right?

As you might imagine, Ryan was beyond overwhelmed. Among other things in his life, his preaching suffered. He had reached a point where he was so bogged down in everything he was required to do that he could not focus for any length of time on his messages. Even though he felt preaching was important, he couldn't dedicate the necessary energy for it to be effective. As a result, he was boring. *Really* boring.

His sermons were the perfect cure for insomnia—a cocktail of unengaging content and altogether unremarkable mediocrity. His intention, of course, was not to become irrelevant. To stop communicating. To stop engaging. That is no preacher's intention.

I would never purposely become ineffective in my preaching. You wouldn't either. But often we slip into a routine and gradually become less and less engaging. Many of us, like Ryan, have so many things to do that we don't give our sermons and our preaching the necessary attention they require. The result: boring, ineffective sermons.

This is an important reality to face when preaching: *Your listeners will get bored.* It will happen. In fact, some people in your church have little to no interest in listening to you. You cannot avoid this reality. But you can do your best to win their attention anyway.

You should be willing to work hard to earn and keep the attention of those who want to listen. By showing up, they have given you the right to speak into their lives. You don't want to waste their time. They got out of bed, got their kids ready, got in their car, found a parking spot, put their kids in children's ministry, and found their way into the auditorium just in time to catch their breath and try to focus on the moment and not the million things on their minds.

Then you come in. If you are boring, it is such an insult. I know this is hard to stomach, but it's true. As the one preaching, you owe it to your people to give them a reason to listen to you. Paul had this attitude in 1 Corinthians 9:22-23: "... I have become all things to all people, that by all means I might save some. I do it all for the sake of the gospel, that I may share with them in its blessings." He was concerned about relating to every kind of person. Paul knew that God was in control, but he also knew that he had a responsibility to do everything possible to engage people where they were.

Whether he was preaching or just living among people, Paul was committed to the end goal—getting the message of the gospel across. He wanted the same thing you and I want, to communicate effectively. To accomplish this he had to do the same thing we have to do today. He had to figure out what made it possible for him to speak into people's lives. He had to discover how to position himself where he could be influential.

It's the same for us. When it comes to preaching we have to be relentless about gaining and keeping peoples' attention. To understand how to make this happen, it is important to know what prevents this from happening. You have to know what makes you boring.

Remember our friend, Ryan, the overwhelmed *senior* pastor and one-man church staff who keeps getting pushed around? He is going on a journey with us throughout this book. We will see his progress as he discovers an effective way to prepare and deliver a sermon and a better way to take care of himself. Your exact situation may be different from Ryan's, mine is, but I hope you will see yourself in his struggles. This will help you map out your own journey to becoming a killer communicator. We will see how he climbed out of the swirling vortex of unengaging sermons.

Before we can see how far he has come, however, we need to know where he started. We will take a look at exactly what Ryan did to be so incredibly boring. Ryan did the same things a lot of preachers who preach boring sermons do.

FOUR EASY STEPS TO BORING SERMONS

We all know there's nothing quite like a good snoozer of a sermon. We've all sat through them. We've probably given them at one point or another. But what exactly does it take to preach a sermon that makes your listeners fall sound asleep? What does it take to defy everyone's ability to pay attention? If you want to know how to deliver a boring sermon that helps your listeners make up for lost sleep while you preach, join Ryan and form these habits. These are the four steps to boring sermons.

Step 1: Do not adequately prepare. The first step to get everyone shutting their eyes is to not prepare. This part is easy. You want to stand up and have absolutely nothing of substance to say. You want to just repeat some things you already know and have already said so your listeners will check out and go to sleep.

Preparation is often the first thing to go when ministry gets overwhelming. Ryan found that other things began creeping into his prep time. This caused him to develop bad habits of "just winging it" and relying on his talents and gifting. Preparing the Sunday sermon on Saturday night became all too common for him. The result was he had nothing to say.

When you do not adequately prepare your sermons, you ensure you will deliver an aimless sermon. Lack of preparation leads most preachers to ramble, to preach longer than they should, and to struggle to define and clearly communicate the point of the sermon. A failure to prepare leads to the next step of preaching boring sermons.

Step 2: Have no clear focus. To preach a boring sermon you should be totally unclear about the direction you want to take the sermon. Your listeners will pick up on this within the first few minutes and decide it's not worth listening because *you* have not figured it out yet. Follow every rabbit trail in your head so your rambling doesn't support your point at all (because you really don't have a point).

Be sure to give an illustration (or two or three) that has no reasonable connection to your sermon. Take people down a disappointing journey of disconnected applications. Make them so frustrated and confused that they give up trying to connect the dots and fall back asleep.

We have all made this mistake before. Early on in my ministry I must have really liked hearing myself talk because I would often ramble without a point. I would take people down a path—a journey of discovery!—and we would figure out together where it ended. You know what I'm talking about, the kind of rambling where you talk yourself into a corner and then keep talking as you try to find your way out, eventually.

This happened almost every week for Ryan. He had no time to think about what his point was going to be on Sunday. He basically just showed up and started talking—a free-flowing monologue from the pulpit. This was not good for him or for Community Church. But he not only lacked focus, he also lacked something else critical to preaching killer sermons: *passion*.

Step 3: Lack passion. If you are too excited about what you are doing you will keep everyone awake. To preach a boring sermon you will want to come across as dull. You should seem somewhat underwhelmed by your content, give the impression it's nothing to get excited about. Make sure all your listeners scratch their heads wondering why you even bothered to get out of bed, much less stand up and preach.

Passion is infectious. Many preaching mistakes are overlooked by a healthy dose of sincere passion. If you bring with you a sense of awe and enthusiasm for your content, your people will catch that enthusiasm. The people who fill your church every week are desperate—in some cases even *dying*—to be inspired. They are eager to be given a sense of hope and reassurance that life can be lived better. When you lack passion you reinforce the feeling some of your people have: "There is nothing in this for me."

Ryan's problem was that he was so tired and so spent by the time Sunday came around he couldn't muster up passion if he tried. Beyond that, because he had no time to prepare he did not feel confident in his sermons by the time he preached them. Any passion he could muster was squelched by insecurity and the fear that any enthusiasm he showed would come across as insincere.

Passion was lacking, and Ryan saw no end to it. His lack of preparation, focus, and passion began to translate into longer and longer sermons because he felt a need to keep preaching so he could eventually find his point and make the sermon worthwhile.

Step 4: Preach too long. If everything else fails to put people to sleep, the clock is on your side. Just keep preaching. Go on and on and on. If the first 30 minutes didn't knock everyone out, try another 10 or 15, maybe even 20. The key is persistence. Don't give up until you are certain the only person listening is you.

I have a lot to say about sermon length (see Chapter 11), but for now suffice it to say that most preachers could stand to preach shorter sermons. Most listeners could stand for their pastor to preach shorter sermons (and couldn't stand the thought of him preaching a longer one.)

But most of us are never at a loss for something to say. We are preachers; we talk. Given the opportunity we will talk for a long time. This gift of gab is what contributes to many boring sermons. (Again, more on that later.)

As Ryan sank deeper and deeper into a preaching rut, his average sermon length actually increased. He started preaching 15-20 minutes over his allotted time each week. The more overwhelmed and unprepared he was, the longer he preached. A lot of us do this when we are not prepared. It seems counter-intuitive, but when we don't know where the sermon is going it takes us longer to get there. It can take a long time to get to nowhere. This is true of you and me, and it was true of Ryan.

This book will walk you through a process of overcoming all four of these common problems and equip you with a tested and proven plan to create and deliver killer sermons.

FROM BORING TO RIVETING

Ryan was in a tough spot. The demands of Community Church had led him to be an unprepared, unfocused, dispassionate, long-winded preacher. In short, he was boring. But was this totally out of his control? Was he merely a passive victim of Community Church and their unrealistic demands? Not at all.

He was only a victim if he chose to be a victim. His schedule, his time, and his priorities were only out of his control if he decided to let them be out of his control. The truth is, Ryan found himself in this awful pattern because *he* let it happen. No one was responsible for the ineffectiveness of his preaching but him.

No one is responsible for the effectiveness of your preaching but you. This means you have to take responsibility for changing the things that need to change in order to become a better communicator.

You and I have a choice, a choice that only we can make. We can either be subject to the unpredictable craziness of ministry, or we can make the most of the situation we are in and become the best possible communicators we can be. My vote is on the latter. Let's explore a killer way to prepare.

LANE SEBRING

PART TWO

KILLER PREPARATION

LANE SEBRING

CHAPTER TWO

Teamwork Makes the Dream Work
A Liberating Approach to Collaborative Preparation

It was Monday morning. Ryan was determined to get started studying for his sermon early this week. Most weeks are so busy that he doesn't have much time to spend on the sermon until later in the week. Thus, sermon preparation eats up most of his weekends.

Ryan sat down at his desk with his computer, his books, his Bible software, and his mind. Some well-meaning people in the church wanted him to preach through Hebrews, so that's what he was doing. He knew what passage the week's sermon would cover, but that's about all he knew.

He was feeling a bit of writer's block. Although it was a passage he had read many times before, after a few hours of study that morning he had no idea where he would take the message. The passage was in Hebrews 4 about Jesus' being our Great High Priest who is able to sympathize with us in our weaknesses.

All Ryan could think about was how that passage related to...*him*. He wasn't thinking of how it would speak to the single mom who is struggling to make ends meet, or the father of four who was recently diagnosed with cancer, or the teenage girl who found out she is pregnant and doesn't know what to do. None of those people crossed his mind.

It is not that Ryan was insensitive. He was just struggling to focus. He needed to get the sermon finished as soon as possible—and to do that, he had to get it started! He didn't have time to consider creative ways to get this message across to a broad range of people. And even if he had the time, he did not quite know where to start.

But one thing he did for sure: He prepared his sermons alone. Like a lot of us, he never once considered any other way of doing it.

THE CHALLENGE OF SOLO PREPARATION

Like Ryan, many preachers prepare their sermons alone. Consider the wisdom in that. Every week you have to get up in front of a group of people and speak words.

Those words have to be engaging, powerful, motivating, encouraging, accurate, practical, and spiritual—all at the same time. Every. Single. Week.

And you prepare alone. *All by yourself.*

This probably started with Moses. He went up on a mountain and heard from God. He came down and told the people, "This is what God said."

In the 3,400 years or so since, we have never really changed the model. Preachers have been preparing sermons alone ever since. I used to prepare my sermons alone. I would read the text, go to commentaries, watch sermons, and research articles, mostly by myself. If you are like most preachers, you prepare alone. The problem is, you and I are not Moses. We are not an Old Testament prophet. There is no requirement that we use this method. Not only that, but Moses had Aaron to help with delivery. So even *he* saw the wisdom in team preaching.

I am not saying that God cannot speak to you in your study. You should hear from God as you prepare. If you have been preaching for any length of time you know how exhilarating it is to spend time in prayer and study and hear from God. There is nothing like it. But this should not lead you to think that you must prepare every sermon alone.

When I went from solo preparation to a team-based model the impact of my sermons improved drastically. They became much more connected to my listeners. I am convinced that a purposeful team approach with intentional input from others at every stage of preparation has been the catalyst for improving my preaching. Before I explain why it works and how to do it, I want to explore the reasons so many of us prepare alone and what drawbacks there are with such a method.

WHY YOU PREPARE ALONE

I can't get inside your head, but I know what I've thought from time to time. And you and I probably have some things in common. There are four likely reasons you prepare your sermons by yourself (in addition to simply following the approach handed down to each succeeding generation of preachers from Moses on):

You want to take the credit. If you hole up for days in a room with books and come up with the most profound truths anyone has ever heard, then you can bask in the glow of your insights. Everyone will be in awe, and *you* will be the star. If you developed content collectively, however, then others may know that not every brilliant insight originated with you.

Preaching plays to our senses of pride and despair. If we do well and others recognize us, we can swell with pride. If we do poorly and others criticize us, we can shrink in despair. Preparing alone sets us up not only for pride but also for despair. (More on this in the Conclusion.) If you want to take all the credit, you have to be prepared to take all the blame.

You think your ideas are the best. Why talk to anyone else when they are not likely to contribute anything you don't already know? Why ask what the interns think of your content? You are the one with the graduate degree in theology. Why ask a group of people to give you feedback before you complete your sermon? They, unlike you, have not been preaching for years.

Nothing will hinder our ability to improve as a preacher more than thinking we have nothing more to learn. If you prepare alone because you suspect that no one else can compete with your ideas, then you are setting yourself up for failure. The truth is: Your ideas improve with input from others.

Your pastor or mentor used to go hide in a room for 20 hours. Perhaps the pastors you learned the most from were committed to spending several hours a week hidden "in their study" to hear from God. This was the assumed method in seminary, and you do not see any need to change things up.

You see it as a more spiritual experience. You are "God's anointed," and unless the message comes from you it won't have the right amount of pastor sauce. After all, if you were to prepare with others, wouldn't that somehow cheapen the process and the *product*?

Perhaps you prepare alone for no other reason than it is just what you do. What could be wrong with that?

Though this is a matter of personal preference, I have found that it is far more beneficial to prepare sermons, at least in part, collaboratively.

WHAT'S THE PROBLEM WITH PREPARING ALONE?

At this point you may be asking: So what if I prepare my sermons alone? What difference does it make?

If almost everyone does it this way, then how could it be so bad? Well, consider this: If you prepare your sermons alone week after week, you draw from the same well, and eventually it will run dry. You start to tell the same stories, use the same examples, select the same Scriptures, and teach in the same way.

You alone prepare sermons that interest *you* on topics that interest *you* for the benefit of ...*others?* Though it doesn't make a lot of sense, it is the standard method of many pastors.

In my case, I would collaborate on so many other areas of ministry. We would meet in teams and plan events or work on strategic direction in the church, and I loved the experience of doing ministry with others! When healthy collaboration happens it is a beautiful thing. But then I would go to my office and sit alone by myself and write my sermon. What I found missing in my solo preparation is all that energy and life from the process of bouncing ideas around with others. It took me a while to see what I was missing when it was just me sitting at my desk staring at a computer screen.

What happens when, week after week, you have prepared your sermons sitting alone in a room with books and a computer? What happens after years and years of limited input from anyone but you? Preparing alone leads to three primary outcomes.

Your sermons lack relational depth. Your messages should be rich with relational insight. The stories, examples, and applications you share should come from a variety of relational experiences. This happens only when you bring other people into the process. You are one person with one set of experiences that are decidedly different from your listeners'.

I benefit tremendously from getting input from people who are not like me. I will talk to a single mom and ask her to give me feedback on something I am planning to preach on family. I will run a concept by a senior citizen to see if it will connect with him or her.

The more input you can get from different kinds of people in different life situations, the better your chance of connecting with more people.

You miss your blind spots. You have blind spots in your life and ministry. We all do. These blind spots show up in your preaching. Developing sermon content can be one of the most vexing things we do as preachers. In the process of praying, studying, and trying to synthesize all your material into a sermon, we can miss things because we have tunnel vision. We can be so consumed in study and so excited about the material that we fail to realize that it will make no sense to most of our listeners.

Including others in the process of sermon preparation keeps us from running with an idea or concept that will not work, is not biblical or is not right for the occasion. It protects you from your blind spots.

It all depends on your hearing from God. Way too much pressure is put on you when you have to come up with all of the sermon content every week. You are not infinitely wise. You cannot possibly know every week exactly what needs to be said. Preparing in a team draws from a pool of greater wisdom. Instead of thinking that just you and you alone need to hear from God, why not have a team of people hearing from God?

HOW TEAM PREPARATION WORKS

I want to give you some practical tools for how to get started preparing your sermons in a team. This practice changed everything about the way I prepare sermons and enriched my preaching experience.

It is important to recognize what constitutes a team. For the purposes of sermon prep, a team could be a structured group that meets regularly or it could be an unstructured assortment of people you seek out to collaborate with. The crucial point is that you are intentionally broadening the preparation process to more than just you.

Our preaching team is made up of our pastors who preach in the main services, the service programming coordinator, other staff members, and a note taker. We meet each week to do four things.

Pray. The most important thing our team does is pray continually for our upcoming services, preaching series, and sermons to be effective and powerful. We recognize that no amount of collaborative planning can replace God's movement among his people. So we pray for Him to use us.

Think and create together. We use the time as an opportunity to bounce ideas around and think together about what kind of teaching content the church needs in the coming weeks and months.

Do long-range sermon series planning. We look at the coming months and plan the teaching series we are going to do. Sometimes this requires a separate meeting for more long-range planning.

Do short-term sermon planning. We typically look at three sermons at a time—the upcoming week and the two weeks that follow. Each pastor who preachers presents the basic flow of their content to the rest of the team. As a team we try to boil down the objective and desired response of the three upcoming sermons (more on objectives and desired responses in chapter 4). This ensures that our goals for the service align with those of the message. It also gives us something to evaluate the following week so we can know whether we hit our target.

When the meeting is over, collaboration continues informally throughout the week. I also seek input from a variety of different people to make sure my content makes sense and communicates what I intend.

HOW TO GET STARTED

Form a structured team. You may be ready to launch a structured team that meets regularly. One great place to start is with the people who are already involved in leading your services: your worship leader, other pastors and staff members, or a lay person who is invested in your church. You may be surprised to find how willing people are to contribute when you let them into the mysterious world of sermon prep.

Make sure your team is composed of individuals who will be okay if you don't use their great idea or research they did for a given sermon. Not every idea can or should make it into the final message. Bringing lots of ideas to the table helps round out your knowledge of the subject even if the ideas aren't presented.

Seek out informal collaboration. You do not need a structured team to begin preparing collaboratively; you can take steps toward it right now. You might have a couple friends at church who like to talk about your sermons.

Ask them if they would be willing to meet with you each week or every other week (in person or virtually) and talk about your upcoming sermon. This is especially helpful to keep in mind if you are the single staff person at your church. Begin with who you have and build it from there.

PHASES OF PREPARATION AND INPUT

Once you have a team together, begin thinking of your preparation in terms of phases and consider what kind of input you can get for each phase along the way.

Before study begins. Discuss your passage or topic with others. Write down the ideas that come to mind from your discussion.

Once you have begun your study. Take what you have from your initial stages of study and bounce it around. Talk to others to see what they have learned from that passage.

After you have a rough outline. Walk someone through your outline and ask for feedback. As you share it out loud with someone else, you will begin to solidify your thoughts.

After your sermon, get feedback to help prepare for the next one. Ask people for meaningful feedback. If it was good, what made it good? If it was bad, what made it bad? (We will explore how to get useful feedback on your sermons in chapter 6.)

My preaching has benefited tremendously from this

method. My sermon gets a great start as I prepare to meet with the team. Its direction is solidified as we think through it together. And as I study I bounce ideas around with a lot of people, which helps me develop a more impactful sermon.

My suggestion is to give it a try and see what happens. You may just find that your sermon prep becomes more fun and your sermons become more effective.

One pastor said that when he tried asking some people in his church for input they told him, "I'm not here to help you write your sermons. That's what we pay you to do!" They responded as if he was being lazy by asking for input from others.

This is an unfortunate response, but one I fear is all too common. I did, however, get a lot of great feedback from preachers who have begun (or already were) doing part of their preparation with other people. Most preachers I talk to who have tried it, love it.

At Community Church, Ryan got started by making a list of three people in his church who would possibly be willing to bounce some ideas around about his sermon. When he reached out to them, they all agreed to begin meeting. Although he was thrilled with this, he still faced a pretty massive challenge—his schedule. No matter what he tried, he could not maintain a consistent schedule. We will look at the issue of scheduling in the next chapter.

CHAPTER THREE

Finding Time to Prepare
How to Take Control of Your Weekly Schedule

In his years of ministry at Community Church, Ryan had never had any kind of predictable schedule. Although in ministry there is no such thing as a "predictable schedule," he just wanted some measure of normalcy. But it was not happening at Community Church.

Ryan loved to preach. Of all the duties his job required, preaching was among the most rewarding. And, yet, among all his varied responsibilities, nothing was more vexing than preparing sermons. With all the other demands on his time, he found it more and more difficult to find time to prepare. He also realized that his sermons were beginning to lack the energy and creativity they had when he first came to the church.

Others began to notice it, too. He would get comments such as: "Brother [they would always begin with "brother" when hurling insults], a lot of us have been talking about how your sermons have just, well ... they're just not as good as they used to be." This frustrated Ryan because he felt as though he could not change his situation. He was a slave to his crazy unpredictable schedule. Preaching was one of the most important things he did for the church, and he was preparing last minute more and more.

He decided to make a change. This was a bold move for Ryan because, to this point, he had let his schedule happen *to* him. He was on the receiving end of everyone else's demands, which of course was not healthy nor was it good leadership. Any system that depends on one person doing everything will eventually crumble. If somehow it does not crumble, it will certainly not grow.

Ryan decided to develop a preaching preparation schedule. He needed to devote specific time each week to developing his sermons. This small change made a huge impact on Ryan's ministry, his time-management, and his sense of accomplishment. This is a change that will certainly benefit your ministry as well. Ryan had to take stock of his weekly responsibilities, move some obligations around, delegate others, and make sermon prep a top priority.

Developing a consistent preparation schedule is something all of us should do, and this chapter will walk you through how to get started.

WHY HAVE A SERMON PREP SCHEDULE?

While preaching is so much fun, preparing can be vexing. Getting up to preach, feeling the energy in the room, sensing the Spirit of God working in you to deliver a message that impacts your listeners—this is great fun. I love it. You love it. It is invigorating. But when I finish preaching on a Sunday, two things are on my mind:

1. I am exhausted, but that was so much fun!

2. I have another sermon to preach in seven days!

I have precious little time to enjoy what God did through one sermon because I have to starting thinking, praying, and preparing for the next one, which is usually seven days away. Those days fly by.

The days leading up to preaching a sermon can be stressful. The responsibility of preparing a sermon is daunting because when Sunday comes you have to deliver. This weight is on your mind all week. Thoughts of what might be relevant to your message are a near constant on your mind.

The key is to have a schedule—a workflow schedule that helps you determine whether you are on track with your preparation. You will experience more freedom in your week leading up to your sermons when you have a plan. I began using a weekly sermon prep schedule a few years ago. It has helped me eliminate some of the stress leading up to a sermon. A weekly prep schedule can do the same for you for a few reasons.

It helps you stay on schedule. As a preacher you never want to procrastinate and put off your sermon prep. But things come up and you have to deal with unexpected events. Your study gets interrupted, and it is difficult to stay on schedule. A written sermon prep schedule is an objective measure. It can help you stay on track because if you get behind, you will know it. If you get ahead, you will know it. Sometimes writing the schedule down is half the battle. This will help you avoid scheduling other meetings on top of your most important preparation times. Additionally, a schedule may reduce the amount of time spent preparing because concentrated study times tend to be more efficient than stop and start study times.

It prevents your sermon prep from becoming all-consuming. It is easy to let the sermon take up your work week. To let it become all you think about. To put other work aside so that you can focus on it exclusively. There are times when the sermon content demands this kind of undivided attention, but if this is your norm then you will have an unbalanced ministry. This is especially true if you not only preach but oversee ministries and staff as well. A leader buried in constant study is an inattentive leader. You want to be able to prepare sermons *and* attend to the needs of your church. A sermon prep schedule allows you to pull away from the study and still be confident that you are on schedule.

A schedule enables you to build margin into your week. All of us need margin in our schedules. We thrive when there is flexibility that enables us to deal with the unexpected. A sermon prep schedule allows you to plan your week in its entirety and keep enough room for the unplanned. If you make sermon preparation part of your non-negotiable weekly tasks then it is less likely to get interrupted or pushed aside for other things.

A SAMPLE PREPARATION SCHEDULE

To simplify this, I have listed out each day of the week with a brief description of what I complete regarding my sermon prep on that day. Every pastor's schedule is different, and every church has its own unique set of meetings and weekly schedules. But I want to share my schedule with you as an example of what one looks like.

Prior to Monday I would have already begun praying and reading through the text. The preaching team would have already developed an objective and desired response for the sermon (more on this in chapter 4). This particular message would fit into a series with its own goals and objectives.

Monday. I begin studying the text in the morning. This includes the initial stages of reading the text several times, making notes of my observations, using commentaries and Bible software study aids, and drafting possible sermon outlines. We have a preaching team meeting in the afternoon to discuss content. I begin the first draft of the sermon outline and notes by the end of the day.

Tuesday. This day includes no official sermon preparation because it is full of meetings, but I have my sermon content in the back of my mind. If I get a moment of inspiration I make sure to write it down.

Wednesday. I study in the morning with the intent of finalizing the first draft of the sermon outline. I record what I have into the voice memo app on my phone. Hearing myself say it out loud helps me develop my thoughts and add meat to the outline.

I begin building the message slides. Creating my own message slides helps me sharpen the focus of my message. As I am thinking of what my listeners will see on the screen, it enables me to do further edits to get down to the best content.

Though I continually seek input from others, I do so especially on Wednesdays. At this point I have developed a workable structure. Thus, I am able to share my content with some people to hear their thoughts, see what might not be clear, and get ideas for illustrations and stories. These people may be members of the preaching team, other staff members, and church members. I have learned that there is no such thing as a bad person to ask because everyone can provide a unique perspective.

Thursday. I finalize my notes in the morning. I get everything on one page before my sermon is ready to go (more on that when I discuss preparing my sermon notes in chapter 5). If I have more than one page, I need to keep editing. I do not use a manuscript but rather my notes, which serve as triggers and summaries. I rarely look at my notes when I preach because my preparation process ensures that by the time I deliver the sermon I have internalized it and am ready to preach it without notes. The notes are there merely as insurance.

I submit notes for the bulletin in the morning on Thursdays. We have a service walk-through with the service planning team in the afternoon to ensure all of our service elements and transitions are properly planned for all three services.

I preach my sermon out loud to an empty room. If anybody walks by while I am doing it, they probably think I've lost my mind because I preach with the same passion as if there were 1,000 people in the room. I have found rehearsing is the best way to know exactly what to expect when I preach the sermon. I click through my slides to make sure they flow naturally with the message.

Using the voice memo app on my phone, I record the message for time and content. I have a 30-minute time-limit on my sermons, and I am committed to sticking to it (more on the importance of time-limits in chapter 11). Recording helps ensure that I meet my time limit. If my rehearsal goes 36 minutes I know I need to cut six minutes from the sermon. To some this may seem a bit obsessive, but it is what makes the difference between preaching "okay" sermons and preaching more effective sermons that pack a tighter punch.

After rehearsing I make necessary adjustments to the content. If a lot of adjustments are needed I record it again. Once I am sure I have the sermon ready to preach, I send off my slides to the media team and feel a great sense of accomplishment.

Friday. I don't even think about the sermon. Not even for a second. Friday is my day off, and I am committed to fully disengaging from the process. I spend time with my family and enjoy the day. The mental break from the sermon actually helps, too, because when I revisit the material on Saturday I am energized by it instead of being tired of it.

Saturday. I review the sermon one more time. I usually listen to my final recording from the last rehearsal I did while clicking through my slides in real time. Sometimes my wife listens with me and pauses the recording when she has a critique, question, or suggestion. She often adds an element of humor as she is great at coming up with funny things to say at the right times. Whenever I use her material it always goes over like crazy.

Sunday. This is the day when I preach the sermon. I

have a routine that includes eating a good breakfast and going over my notes, which I will discuss in detail in chapter 10.

Given that I spend time on preparation most days of the week, you may wonder where I get the time. Simply put, I carve it out and set the expectation. Monday and Wednesday mornings are off-limits except unavoidable meetings or emergencies. As much as possible, I avoid meetings, emails, and phone calls and use those mornings to study and make progress on the sermon. Then I'm free to focus on other important ministry in the afternoons.

Thursdays are not so intense because by then I am usually only putting on finishing touches. I structure it this way because I do not want to be writing my sermon on Saturday night. I am determined to get it done during the week and have a life outside of sermon prep. I also believe it produces a much better product when I complete it a few days before delivering because I have the time to really let it sink into my heart and mind.

When you develop your schedule, make sure to communicate it to everyone you work with and anyone else who has a claim on your time. Block the time out on your calendar and make it a priority. That brings us to the application step. It is your turn to make a schedule.

HOW TO MAKE A SCHEDULE

As you begin making your schedule it is helpful to

address a few questions.

What other meetings already happen that you will need to work around? If you have meetings all day Monday, perhaps it makes sense to begin your study on Tuesday. If you have morning meetings but free afternoons on most days, then afternoons may work better. If you find that your current meeting schedule is overwhelming and impairs your productivity, take steps to change it.

When are you at your best? I am the most productive, alert, and creative during the morning hours. This is why I make time for study in the mornings and do meetings in the afternoons. The intense focus sermon prep requires demands morning time for me. You may not be at your best in the mornings, so carving out some time in the afternoons may be the best solution for you.

What deadlines do you have to meet? If your church issues a paper bulletin, when does it get printed? When are your slides due? If your message gets translated into other languages, when are those notes due to the translators? If you do not have deadlines for these, you might want to consider making self-imposed deadlines to help keep you on schedule. Work them into your prep schedule so they are milestones that help keep you on track. My slides are not "due" by Thursday afternoon, but I get them in by then because it forces me to complete them by the time I have set.

When is your day off? You never want your sermon

prep to bump into your day off. Protect your day off as though it is something you could lose if you aren't careful. Because it is. My day off is Friday, so I arrange my schedule to ensure I am finished with the sermon prep on Thursday. If you do not have a day off, you should fight to get one. (More on the importance of having a day off in chapter 12.)

How far ahead do you need to work to feel like you are on top of things? Everyone takes a different approach. Some are okay with preparing for a sermon the week it is to be delivered. Others need to be weeks ahead. Still others are comfortable being a week and a half ahead. The key is to discover what you are most comfortable with and make your schedule fit.

Answer these questions and any others that come to mind, and then begin thinking through your prep steps. Write down everything you do to prepare a sermon from start to finish. Think in detail from the time you first look at the text until you preach it. Once you have your list, begin breaking it down into when you could do each task in the order that you would do it. Write down a first draft of a schedule and give it a shot. Adjust it as the weeks go by, and you will find that in two to three weeks you have an accurate idea of what your schedule should entail. When you've completed this process, write it down and share it with anyone who needs to know (such as fellow staff, ministry team members and your spouse).

A PREDICTABLE WEEK? NO WAY!

You may be thinking, *Yeah, a prep schedule sounds great in a fantasy world, but in real life it is impossible!* I agree that some contexts make it more difficult to establish a schedule—if you are doing bi-vocational ministry for example. But don't declare it impossible while accepting other burdens on your schedule without even thinking about it.

One person commenting on an article I wrote on this topic had this to say:

"And when does the sermon finally get prepared, and what happens if you have two sermons to get ready for Sunday and a Bible study before then and a few shorter services during the week; a denominational all day-er on Tuesday and a surprise elders meeting thrown in at one of your farthest flung churches on Friday morning? This also in addition to some sarcastic remarks that someone has been home from the hospital for a month and still hasn't seen the minister!"

This person's situation may seem all too familiar to you. I am not suggesting that it is easy to have a sermon prep schedule, but that it is very important, so important in fact that you should work to make whatever changes are necessary to develop and maintain a schedule. If the schedule in the previous comment is representative of a typical week for you, then you are doing too much. That is the kind of schedule that leads a lot of pastors to burn out.

What other leaders can you build up to take some of

that load off of you? Do *you* need to teach that Bible study or could someone else do it? If you have two different sermons on Sunday, could someone else preach the other one? If people are ambushing you with surprise meetings, could you ask them to respect your boundaries and plan them out better in advance? Could another ministry leader or pastor visit the person in the hospital?

If your church depends on you to preach every sermon, teach every Bible study, be present at (or even preside over) every meeting, and visit every sick person in the hospital, then I can certainly see why the thought of having a schedule frustrates you. I would work on changing the culture in your church to be more of an equipping culture that empowers others rather than relying solely on you.

To consistently prepare and deliver killer sermons, you must establish, protect, and follow a schedule. You are not a victim of anyone's demands. Make your priorities clear and then be reasonable and stick to them. If your church does not honor your desire to study God's Word carefully so you can proclaim it effectively, then do everything you can to change your church culture. You owe it to the people you serve, to yourself and to the pastor who will eventually follow you.

Ryan was able to change the cultural landscape at Community Church when it came to the demands they put on his time. They wanted better sermons, and he needed more time. He communicated this need and was rewarded with the space and time necessary to adequately prepare his sermons.

But even with more time on his hands, Ryan found himself challenged with the same dilemma you and I face: He was not sure what his sermons were supposed to *do*. Sure, he had plenty of time to study, but what was the point? More specifically, what was the point of his sermons? More on this in the next chapter.

CHAPTER FOUR

Every Sermon Needs a Job
Putting Your Sermon to Work

As a church we were preaching through the Gospel of John. I was excited because John is one of my favorite Gospels. John's admonition to his readers to believe in Jesus is one of the most basic, yet profound declarations we preachers make. Like John, we ask people to believe. We ask them to stop trusting in themselves and trust in Jesus. Easy enough, right? I thought it would be easy until I got to a passage that I loved, John 1:14-18.

And the Word became flesh and dwelt among us, and we have seen his glory, glory as of the only Son from the Father, full of grace and truth. (John bore witness about him, and cried out, "This was he of whom I said, 'He who comes after me ranks before me, because he was before me.'") For from his fullness we have all received, grace upon grace. For the law was given through Moses; grace and truth came through Jesus Christ. No one has ever seen God; the only God, who is at the Father's side, he has made him known.

This passage is so rich with content about Jesus' humanity. About His incarnation. It is a passage that celebrates God becoming man. It demonstrates God's great love for humanity in that he would send his Son to become one of us and live among us. When we look at Jesus we see the Father. Amazing. Astounding...

Until you try to preach about it. When I sat down and began studying this passage it was a thrilling process. There is so much truth in this short text that volumes and volumes have been written about it. I made a number of observations and conclusions about the text, read several chapters of several books, and watched sermons. At the end of this I had pages of notes on this passage. This is the fun part.

Then I had to take all this raw material and shape it into a finished product—a killer sermon. Ever been there? Of course you have. For most of us this happens every time we preach. The richer and more amazing the passage, the more in-depth we study, the more material we have, and the harder it is to decide where to take the sermon.

After all my study of this passage, I had to decide what was most important for *that* sermon. There are plenty of resources available that will teach you how to do this from a technical perspective. If you have not studied biblical hermeneutics, which is the art and science of biblical interpretation, I suggest that you do that to provide some helpful background knowledge of how to handle the text appropriately.

Even when you know how to properly handle a text and not misuse its meaning, however, it is still difficult to determine what makes it into a sermon. Beyond that, from a communication perspective, you have to consider what your audience needs and how much they can handle.

I knew as I looked over this material that I was not going to be able to cover even one-tenth of what I had studied. If I tried it would be like giving my listeners a sip of water from ... a fire hose. Unfortunately some preachers take this approach. They get all the information they can and then unload it on their people. It may make them feel good to disseminate mountains of information every week, but when they are finished their people cannot remember most of it. They leave knowing they heard a sermon, but without much more. They may even make comments such as, "Wow, that was really deep." Which is code for, "I didn't really get it; I have nothing to apply; but I'm sure it was good."

But there has to be an uncomplicated way to take what you have studied and begin drilling down to where you want to take it this week. There must be a way to simplify the approach without losing the richness of the message. You have to move beyond the material itself and begin thinking about what you want to accomplish with it.

It was helpful for me to begin thinking of my sermons in terms of what they *do*. My sermon is active. It is not neutral. It has an opinion, it motivates, it inspires, it ignites passion in people. The sermon must have a job, and it must do its job. Of course, God is the One who uses the sermon, but killer communicators do their part to remove distractions and make it as effective as possible.

In the John passage, I had to rise above my study to think about what I wanted the sermon to do. This was my sermon's *objective*. Then I had to think about what I wanted my people to do with the sermon. This was the *desired response*. My preaching team and I developed a process to help us establish an objective and desired response to bring clarity to every message.

I want to walk you through this process so you can determine what to focus on with every message. Implementing this approach will help you assess whether your sermon worked after you preached it. Before you can know if you were successful, you have to know what you were seeking to accomplish. This is true in every area of life but especially in preaching. This is why I nail down two questions before every sermon. These two questions are an essential part of my sermon preparation process because they bring clarity to every sermon.

1. What is the objective for this sermon? When you think back on a sermon you have preached, you should know whether you met your objective. Nothing is more frustrating than putting lots of work into a sermon and having no way to measure its effectiveness. To assess the sermon, however, you need an objective to measure it against. And to meet an objective, you must *have* an objective. So what exactly is a preaching objective?

A preaching objective is simply what you want the sermon to *do*. A sermon should be more of a verb than a noun. A sermon should work. It should accomplish things. But your sermon only accomplishes what you make it accomplish. Your sermon only works as hard as you do. It is essential to understand exactly what you want your sermon to do before you preach it. This is your preaching objective.

Example objectives: This sermon will:
- Show how knowing your identity in Christ makes a difference in your relationships
- Teach people how to pray
- Demonstrate how God has worked all throughout history
- Show how this Old Testament passage points to

Jesus
- Show how to understand and apply this passage of scripture
- Teach people what biblical giving looks like and how to do it

Every sermon needs a purposeful objective. If you have not clearly defined the objective for your sermon, you will not know whether you have hit it. The objective is not the same as a main point. Your point(s) should correspond to your objective, but your objective rises above your point to another level. The objective is what your sermon does, while your point is what your sermon teaches. Sometimes these are closely related, but they answer two different questions.

Developing a sermon objective. To decide on an objective, I ask some questions during my preparation.

- What is the point of this text?
- What is the theme of this preaching series?
- What am I trying to get across?
- What is the most important truth for them to remember?
- What matters most for *this* sermon?
- What is *not* as important for *this* sermon?

These questions help me narrow down exactly what I want my sermon to do. Before I get too far in my preparation, I write down the objective. This is typically one of the first things we do in the preaching team meeting after discussing the text itself.

Nailing down an objective is important, but it is incomplete without the accompanying application. Your sermon needs a desired response. This leads to the second question I ask of every sermon I prepare.

2. What is the desired response for this sermon? What is a desired response? If the objective is what your *sermon* is to *do*, the desired response is what your *listeners* are to *do* with the sermon. If the sermon works as it is supposed to, your listeners will know exactly what they are to do in response. Put another way, a desired response is how you want your sermon to be applied.

To set a desired response, define ahead of time what it looks like to apply your message. If your sermon objective is met, the response will complement it perfectly.

A desired response helps ensure your listeners walk away from your sermon knowing exactly how they can apply the message to their lives. The proof is in the doing, so you can only know your sermon worked when you see it resulting in life-change.

Example desired responses: When people walk away from this sermon they will:

- Take a step toward living in light of their identity in Christ
- Begin an intentional daily prayer time
- Understand God's redemptive work in history

and trust him with their future
- Embrace how all of life points to Jesus and his redeeming work
- Study this passage further and apply it to their lives
- Begin giving financially to their local church

Creating a desired response. To create a desired response, I ask some questions of the sermon.

- What would it look like to apply this text?
- How would my life be different if I actually believed this?
- What is the most important step to take to apply this message?
- How does this message hit home in people's lives?
- How does this message challenge, convict, motivate, or comfort people?

Desired responses are flexible. God works on different people in different ways through the same message. So I am not disappointed if someone applies my message in a way other than I desired. In fact, there may be dozens of ways to apply a message. The important consideration is whether the sermon is making a difference, even if the progress is incremental.

The desired response is a preparation aid. Think of it this way: If you know what your message could look like if someone put it on like a jacket and wore it out, then it will help you prepare with the end in mind.

For every sermon I preach, I nail down the objective and the desired response as part of my preparation process. This initial stage is accomplished in the preaching team meeting.

The objective and desired response are mostly for you to know. I am not suggesting you get up and say, "Okay, everyone my objective is _____ and my desired response is _____." That would most likely produce a collective yawn. When you have clearly defined your objective and desired response, they will come out in your message. You do not have to announce them. They will work themselves out naturally as you preach in a way that matches your objective and aims at your desired response.

On the other hand, if you do not have an objective, your listeners will know this. If you do not know how your sermon could be applied, your listeners probably won't know either. You must know these two things and be confident in them. This is why I make answering these two questions a top priority early on in my prep process. As I move later in my preparation, I focus on three tests that let me know if my sermon is ready to preach.

TESTS TO ENSURE THE SERMON IS READY

For every sermon you preach, you should be absolutely clear what you want your people to take away from it. If you are murky about how they will be able to use your message, then you can be sure they will be clueless. Not to mention that they will pick up on your uncertainty and check out because their time is valuable and you have chosen to waste it.

Preachers who want to communicate well must make clarity a top priority in every sermon. But it is easy, and sometimes necessary, to focus most of your prep time on your content and not on your listeners. This makes it so crucial to think through how your listeners will receive and use your message. I use three simple tests to ensure that my sermon is ready to go in terms of its impact on my listeners and their ability to apply it.

This is drop-dead simple, and it is meant to be. At this point in your prep you have already done the complicated work of establishing your objective and desired response. Now comes the icing on the cake that helps you ensure a strong, focused delivery that accomplishes what you want. These three tests did not originate with me. They are as standard as it gets, but so very helpful. They will be another tool you can put to use easily as you prepare.

The three things that must be clear before your sermon is ready to preach are what you want your listeners to know, feel, and do because of your sermon.

1. What you want your listeners to know (information). When you get up to preach you need to be clear about what information you want to get across. In Romans 12, the Apostle Paul says that we are to be transformed by the renewing of our minds. This means that the Word of God should continually be changing the way we think. Your sermon is one of the building blocks of this transformation for your people.

People cannot remember everything you say, but they can remember *some* of it. You should determine what is the most important thing you are saying and ensure you communicate it clearly. For your listeners to walk away knowing what you want them to know, you must avoid information overload.

It's helpful to boil your message down to a cohesive, simple, easy-to-remember statement that your listeners can walk away with. Some call this the nail to hammer, the bottom line, or the big idea.

Call it whatever you want; it is effective. Take the one overarching truth that sums up your message and craft it into a single statement. Here are a couple examples from some of my recent sermons:

- *To not just survive, but thrive, be connected to the Vine.*
- *Peace does not come from perfect circumstances but from faith in a perfect Savior.*
- *The peace of God is bigger than your storms.*

You do not have to kill yourself making them clever. If they are concise and repeatable, they will do the trick. There is another test to consider, however, because information transfer is not enough. People can know what they need to know and yet be completely comfortable doing nothing with it. There is more to preaching than making ideas clear.

2. *What you want your listeners to feel (inspiration).* How will your sermon connect with people's hearts? Think of the sermons that have had the greatest impact on you. You probably remember not only the facts that were taught but the way it made you *feel*. It was not the facts but the powerful story beautifully told that truly moved you. Your listeners are the same! They want to be moved at an emotional level. They want to be inspired, to be lifted up, to be encouraged, to be challenged.

You should determine exactly how they should feel as a result of your sermon and aim to create that feeling. (We will examine ways to connect with the emotions and feelings of your listeners in more detail in chapter 9.)

3. *What you want your listeners to do (application).* You need to put handles on your messages that people can grab onto. You must make crystal clear what it looks like for people to apply your message in real life. This is your desired response, and you must deliver your message so that it is clear and applicable.

Sermons must have all three of these elements to be effective. Information without inspiration is boring. Inspiration without application is useless. Here is a simple equation to make sense of it all: Information + Inspiration + Application = Killer Sermon.

Ryan began implementing this method at Community Church. He taught himself to nail down an objective and desired response for every sermon during the initial stages of preparation. He also made it a habit to run his sermon through the three tests of *know*, *feel*, and *do*. Like most of us, however, Ryan still had trouble structuring his message. Where do all the parts fit? In what order? Ryan still needed to work on his sermon outlines. We will explore that in the next chapter.

LANE SEBRING

CHAPTER FIVE

Building Blocks
Outlines, Illustrations, and Application

Ryan has come a long way. He has developed a preaching team and stopped trying to prepare alone. He has established a sermon prep schedule and guards it intensely. He makes sure he is crystal clear on the objective and desired response of every sermon. When it comes to putting it all together in a cohesive flow, however, he is still sometimes at a loss for how to do it. How should he introduce the sermon? How should he order his main points? How should he wrap it up? He has a bottom line, his sermon has an objective, and he knows what it looks like to apply it, but organizing the material is a challenge.

I can relate to Ryan because I have experienced his dilemma. I am sure you have, too. In this chapter, I will share a method for outlining sermons that maximizes impact and communication. This method helped me overcome the dilemma. It is adaptable to your personality and communication style but the general principles apply to all of us. As we explore the method, let's keep three important ideas in mind.

Outline in a way that fits you. Your method should accommodate your distinct personality, style, and comfort level. For example, although I have never used a manuscript because doing so would not work with my personality and presentation style, I've seen preachers use them well. The key is to find what works for you.

Each sermon is different, so the approach will vary. Some sermons are part of a series where the thread of a major idea runs through each sermon. Other sermons are more standalone, topical sermons that deal with a given issue. Still others may answer a question or explain an aspect of doctrine. In any case, consider the implications of the type of sermon you are preparing and factor that into your outlining method.

Each audience is different and has varying needs. The key here is context. Consider the people you are speaking to and factor in their specific life-stages, needs, educational levels, backgrounds, and preferences. Communication is about the listener, so you should avoid having a one-size-fits-all approach to sermon structure.

With these cautions in mind, let's discover a killer

way to structure killer messages.

A METHOD FOR OUTLINING SERMONS

I have adopted a method from a variety of techniques I have observed, studied, and experimented with over the years. From my trial-and-error, I have developed a method that seeks to combine the best of all practices. It has four basic steps.

Step One: Present the Problem. Begin your sermon by presenting a problem and helping everyone see they have a stake in it. You want to make every listener know that your sermon is going to be helpful and add value to his or her life. Perhaps they should be interested regardless, but this is not usually the case. Your job as the preacher is to get their attention. If you can winsomely articulate a problem that everyone feels, your listeners will be more likely to give you an ear.

This concept could also be called *building tension*, an idea that Andy Stanley developed extensively in his book *Communicating for a Change: Seven Keys to Irresistible Communication*. Put simply, building tension involves getting your listeners interested in the content before you start teaching it. It takes creativity and hard work to think through exactly how to foster interest in your content. Before you begin teaching through a text, get your listeners on the hook for what you are about to preach.

The problem must matter to them. Though this is

sometimes referred to as a "felt need," most people do not readily feel felt needs. Your job is to get them to see that it is a problem. You can sometimes do this by presenting it in the form of a question. Other times you will present it as a statement that everyone can relate to. Either way, discuss a real problem that people really feel (or should feel).

Here are some examples of common problems a sermon can address. The problem that we pursue peace in all kinds of things that do not give it. Or that we have a distorted view of God and don't really believe he is good. Or that we have idols and consequently give ourselves to hobbies, pursuits, and passions in a way that mirrors worship. Or that we are barely scraping by in our finances, health, relationships, or jobs.

Whatever the problem, build tension by presenting it and massaging it until everyone feels it. Because even if there are some in your audience who are not feeling exactly what you are describing, they will know someone who is. Do not stop asking the questions and presenting the problem until everyone is on the hook for the solution.

This method works whether you are preaching through a passage exegetically or covering a topic. The vast majority of my preaching is expository through books of the Bible. As a preaching team we break books down into sections and package each section into a singular focus. These usually become four or five-week series. This makes it easy to determine what the felt need will be for each series and, therefore, each message. To give an example, we recently preached through the Gospel of John. All along the way we broke John into individual series that focused on a central theme. Here is an example of the different series we developed through three chapters of John.

Comfort Zone. This was the series title for John 14. Jesus was speaking to his disciples hours before he was captured and crucified. In the midst of their uncertainty, he reassured them that he provides lasting comfort. For our series and each message in it, we began with the problem we all have of looking for our comfort in everything but Jesus. We are seeking to be comfortable by the world's standards, all the while ignoring the lasting comfort that can come only from Jesus.

Thrive. In this series through John 15, in which Jesus spoke to his disciples about how being connected to the Vine is the only way to bear fruit. The problem we presented was that we settle for merely surviving in life rather than thriving. We are satisfied living mediocre lives when we could be living for so much more.

God in You. In John 16, Jesus promised his disciples that the Holy Spirit would come. This was to reassure them that in his absence they would not be without God, but the Holy Spirit would be with them and in them. The problem we presented in this series was that most of us know a lot *about* God but are not truly *experiencing* his presence. We should be filled with his Spirit and hearing his voice but often we do not and wonder why our lives are so powerless.

You can see that each message or series calls for something different. Every text or topic points to a problem: a failed view, a misaligned hope, a misplaced worship. As you prepare, think through what problem the text is solving and begin by describing it.

You may be asking why there needs to be a problem. Think of the problem in the sermon like conflict in a story. A story is only interesting when there is conflict. If I wrote a novel about a man who had a great life where he overcame no obstacles, had no challenges and faced no opposition, I doubt my novel would be read and shared by anyone. For a sermon to pique the interest of your listeners it needs to present a relatable problem—otherwise it may be sound and true, but uninteresting.

Step Two: Solve the Problem with the Text. After you present the problem and build tension, point your listeners to the text for the solution. When you present the text as the answer it teaches people to look into the Word of God to find answers to life's questions. Ultimately, the answer is Jesus. He is the solution, the answer, the relief, the healing, and the Savior everyone needs. Taking people to the text empowers them to know the heart of God, understand the Gospel, and live in light of it.

Going back to our example of the three series in John 14-16, let's look at how the problem was solved with the text in each series.

Comfort Zone. The problem: We look for our comfort in everything but Jesus. The solution: Jesus told us to find our peace in Him. This is a simplification, and in the sermons we went into more depth and preached the passages holistically, but the general idea was to drive home the idea that Jesus provides lasting comfort and peace.

Thrive. The problem: We settle for surviving in life rather than thriving. The solution: Abide in him and be connected to the Vine. Do nothing apart from Jesus' work in our lives.

God in You. The problem: Most of us know a lot *about* God but are not truly *experiencing* his presence. The solution: Believe what Jesus said about the Holy Spirit—that he would bring to our remembrance what Jesus said, help us, and guide us into all truth. In other words, the solution is to experience God's presence by being filled with the Spirit.

Step Three: Equip the listener to apply it. After walking through the text, give your listeners the tools to apply it. This is where you make your points and give illustrations that help make sense of them (we will explore how to create and use illustrations effectively later in this chapter). This is *not* a list of possible applications. It is better to make your points action-oriented so that the points themselves are applications. Every point should demonstrate how to apply what the text teaches. Be drop-dead practical and teach how living out the text enables your listeners to experience the hope, healing, and answers that everyone was on the hook for at the beginning of the sermon.

Looking again at our example of John 14-16, let's see how the listener was equipped to apply each principle.

Comfort Zone. The problem: We look for our comfort in everything but Jesus. The solution: Jesus told us to find our peace in Him. The equipping: make a practice of going to Jesus with doubts, fears, and anxieties. We consulted scriptures that point to this idea and presented illustrations of what it looks like to trust Jesus in the midst of uncertainty.

Thrive. The problem: We settle for surviving in life rather than thriving. The solution: stay connected to Jesus, the Vine. The equipping: stay connected to Jesus through prayer, community with others, and a life walking with God. We used illustrations about being connected to Jesus to demonstrate what a connected, abiding life looks like.

God in You. The problem: We know a lot *about* God but are not truly *experiencing* His presence. The solution: To believe what Jesus said about the Holy Spirit being in us. The Equipping: Scriptures that teach about the Holy Spirit's work in our lives. We used illustrations about being filled with his presence and living empowered lives.

If I could add a step 3(b) it would go here. At this point in the message it is so important, and so appropriate, to point to the gospel of Christ as the only way we can live life for God. All our efforts to apply any message devolve to moralism without the empowering work of the gospel within us. Every passage points to Jesus' work on the cross as the means by which we are capable of living for him. To miss this is a devastating mistake.

This step is a perfect place to share the gospel because if you are speaking of living it out and being equipped to apply the message, what better place to include the precious truth of Christ in you, the hope of glory (Colossians 1:27). It is Christ in you and through you that empowers you to live for him. This leads to the fourth and final step.

Step Four: Cast vision and inspire. This is where you paint a picture of what it could look like if your listeners applied the truth you have communicated. This involves casting a vision of how different your church would be if everyone actually lived out this life-changing message. It shows how much freer your listeners would feel if they embraced this liberating truth. It demonstrates how much more of an impact you could make on your community if each person submitted fully to God.

Your listeners are desperate to be inspired. They need you to show them that it is possible, it matters, and if they take Jesus at his word and do what he says, it will make a difference because it is simply and absolutely the best way to live. The key word to focus on is *imagine*. Imagine what it would be like if we lived this way. Imagine the impact we would have on the world around us. Imagine…

Let's take a look at how this fits into John 14-16.

Comfort Zone. Imagine what it would be like if while the whole world is anxious and worried, we were in perfect peace because our trust was truly in Jesus.

Thrive. Imagine if we stopped settling for mediocre lives in which we were barely scraping by and started thriving. What would God do through a group of people who were truly connected to him?

God in You. Imagine if we didn't just know *about* God but experienced his presence every day. How much more would our lives be filled with God's power and presence?

You can see that simply using the word imagine or a propositional statement such as "what if we all did this," you can allow your listeners to see, maybe for the first time, that there is hope and that with God's help they can do anything.

These four steps are what I use almost every time I prepare and preach a sermon. I did not develop this out of thin air. Rather, this method is an adaptation of what others have taught. For further reading on similar methods that I have learned and adapted, see Andy Stanley's *Communicating for a Change: Seven Keys to Irresistible Communication* and Lawrence Richards and Gary J. Bredfeldt's *Creative Bible Teaching*.

DEVELOPING NOTES TO HAVE WITH YOU WHILE YOU PREACH

Once you have an outline you need to determine what will be in front of you when you preach.

What do I take in the pulpit with me? This is something I am curious about every time I watch a preacher delivering a sermon. I am always thinking *What's on that piece of paper? What's in that notebook? What's on that iPad?* If I don't spot any notes I am thinking, *Are they hidden where I just can't see them? Are there confidence monitors with queues? A tele-prompter?* I want to know!

I will share how I do notes and what I take with me onto the stage. Because I am always tweaking my approach to sermon notes, these will likely change over time. My notes now look different from how they looked a year ago. I have developed my system over the years to be best for me. My method may not work for you, but the idea is to learn from it and adapt it to develop a method that works best for you.

Here are the basic elements of the notes I have with me while I preach.

One page. I make all of my notes fit on one page. I take a standard Microsoft Word document and set up the page so that it is landscape orientation with two columns and .4" margins, size 11 font. Anything that does not fit on that page does not make it into the sermon.

In my Bible. I put the notes in my Bible. I do not use an iPad because I like the optics of having a paper Bible. Again, if you prefer an iPad because it works better for you then by all means use one. I have a string around the spine of my Bible that holds my notes in so that I am not fumbling around with papers on stage. I simply open my Bible and my notes are ready.

Headers and summaries. I break my notes down into headers and summaries to serve as triggers for my memory. The headers are bold-face and typically contain just the first few words of the thought. It helps me to look down and see what the next thought is quickly so I can speak on the idea. Unless I am reading the text, however, I rarely look at my notes. They are only there if I need them.

Color coded. I color-code each element to make sure I can easily know where I am, whether it is a main point, supporting idea, illustration, reference, application point, and so on.

Texts. Main texts and supporting texts are always printed. It is important to me to have my passage and my cross references included in my printed notes so I never have to flip around in my Bible while I am preaching. This removes an unnecessary distraction and time waster.

Slide queues. I include a reminder of when to advance my slides. This is helpful to me because I advance my own slides with a small remote, but I would also recommend this if someone else is advancing your slides.

ALLITERATIONS ARE ALMOST ALWAYS ABSOLUTELY ATROCIOUS

In the many different styles of outlining, one sticks out and is worth noting—alliterations. Some preachers alliterate their outlines making all their points begin with the same letter. Sometimes just the main points are alliterated; other times the sub-points are alliterated; and still other times the sub-sub-points are alliterated. At one point, preachers were taught that alliteration was a great way to organize a message and really get listeners to remember. *To make it great, alliterate!* was the mantra. But we don't see as much alliteration anymore. I think alliterated outlines are almost always absolutely atrocious. Why?

They make your message seem contrived. Alliterated outlines can appear contrived and forced. As though the preacher just needed a matching, neat outline, he grabbed whatever word fit the others regardless of whether it was actually the best word that communicated the meaning he wanted. Here's an example.

God wants three things from you:

1. Surrender
2. Service
3. Supplication

Seriously, *supplication?* "Prayer" would work just fine here. And more people would know automatically what it means.

Some alliterations can seem crowded and overly complicated. I have read pulpit commentaries that teach pastors how to alliterate several words in a line and make each subsequent line a parallel matching line. Here's an example from a sermon I heard once.

A genuine disciple is:
1. Committed to a pure life.
2. Consistent in their personal life.
3. Constrained by the purpose of life.
4. Convinced of their position in life.

In addition to seeming painfully contrived, this is a complicated mess to navigate through. If we can learn anything from companies such as Google, it is that simplicity rules the day. A wordy, crowded, alliterated outline makes it difficult to navigate what is most important for your listeners to remember.

They do not communicate authenticity. This is because it does not seem like a real conversation. We don't speak to each other in neat, alliterated sentences. As a preacher delivering a sermon you have to work hard to establish a connection—an authentic connection—with your audience. Don't make this harder on yourself by developing an outline that does not seem real because it is *not* real.

Every rule has an exception. Alliteration is not technically the problem. Overuse of alliteration and forced alliteration are the problems. Sometimes it can be very helpful. Other times it is a huge distraction. In my view, what makes the difference is whether memorizing it will help your audience when they walk away. If memorizing the outline is not something that would help them, then there is no need to alliterate.

For instance, if you were preaching on three ways God wants us to love him your outline could be Head, Heart, and Hands. "God wants us to love him with our minds (head). He wants our full emotions (heart). And he wants us to serve him (hands)." It is simple and could be very useful to your listeners.

This can be overused, too. And if you use it too much or in a forced way, it can also be a distraction. So I am careful not to use a device such as alliteration too much.

HOW TO USE ILLUSTRATIONS

As a preacher you want to make your ideas come alive. When you labor preparing a message and perfectly craft your points you are not thinking, *I am sure this will be altogether unremarkable, but I'll give it a try.* No! Instead, you are thinking, *How can I make them see this and feel it and be changed by it?*

We all want this because what good is it if you make a great point but no one feels it? If no one does anything with it? An effective illustration is the secret sauce that makes your listeners grab onto your ideas on an emotional level. A good illustration will reach out and grab your listeners and pull them into your content. It will help you establish an emotional connection and make them care.

So how do you use illustrations effectively? There are plenty of resources on where to find illustrations, but I want to talk about how to use them. You can have a killer illustration, but if you misuse it, it will fall flat. You can give a great illustration at the wrong time and have it lose its punch. You can have an amazing story that you tell poorly, or an interesting analogy that doesn't quite fit, or a metaphor that you fail to connect to your point.

I have made all of these mistakes. You may have, too. Given the complexity and importance of using illustrations, I want to offer some guidance.

Think through the timing and placement. Every time you make a point in a message you want to do three things: explain it, apply it, and illustrate it. Every point is different, and everyone has a different way of communicating an idea, but these three elements basically encompass everything you do with a point. So how do you sequence them?

The key is to find what works for you and for your

listeners. Maybe you explain the point in a teaching format, then once you have laid the foundation you move to illustrating how it works. At the end you flow naturally into application. Or maybe you present the idea without much explanation, but then jump into a story that is going to connect to the idea once you explain it. The point is that there is more than one way to do it, but you need to be intentional about the process for each point.

Though illustrations can work in a lot of areas, you should think through and plan for the best placement. How do you know what's best? Practice out loud a few times. Make your point, explain it, apply it, and illustrate it. Each time you practice, change up the order to see what flows the most naturally. Though I plan out in advance where illustrations will go, I sometimes change it up in the moment. The process of thinking it through ahead of time allows me to adjust it in the moment and still know exactly how it fits.

Jump right into it. Howard Hendricks used to poke at preachers who would give an introduction to their illustrations. Maybe you have heard preachers do this: "And now I'm going to illustrate this point, it's going to be very illustrative, it will serve as an illustration for you to remember."

If you give this wordy, unnecessary introduction, then your illustration is probably dead before you even get started.

Just say it. Just tell the story. Just give the example. Just give the illustration. There is no need to introduce it. Your listeners' brains are working much faster than your mouth is moving. They will connect the dots if the illustration is effective and makes sense. It is much more interesting to move right into a story, example, metaphor, or analogy than to spend precious time setting it up.

Be sure it reasonably connects to your point. If you have to force-fit an illustration to get it to connect to your point, don't use it. It's like telling a joke and then having to explain the punchline. The joke is no longer funny. It never was. If you have to map out how the illustration connects at every level, it has already lost its potency. The illustration is supposed to give your ideas clarity, so if instead it confuses and leaves your listeners scratching their heads trying to connect the dots, the illustration has defeated its purpose.

If you want to be sure it connects, test it out ahead of time. Run it by your preaching team and get feedback.

Make it interesting. Very few things are worse than a boring illustration. Part of the reason you use an illustration is to regain your listeners' attention. If the illustration is uninteresting you miss an opportunity to bring everyone back to focusing on your message.

Avoid giving canned illustrations you find in books and online resources. It takes a lot of work to deliver most of these in a way that doesn't seem contrived. Rather, look for real-life stories, examples, and events. Personal stories almost always deliver, but vary your approach and keep them fresh. Your preaching team comes in handy when you begin telling the same stories too often. Their job is to give you that feedback, your job is to listen.

THE ART OF APPLICATION

Information without application is education. If your goal is simply to educate or inform your audience so they are more knowledgeable about the Bible, then stop preaching.

Preaching of necessity requires application. We are preaching for life-change. We are preaching to make the written Word become the living word in people's daily lives. Your job as a preacher is to show your listeners what it looks like to live out the truths you are presenting from the Scriptures.

Show how the truth of Scripture works in the lives of your listeners. A simple, but effective way to do this is to ask questions. Draw from your point and ask questions that cause your listeners to wrestle with whether or not their lives align with the truth you have proclaimed from the Scriptures.

Avoid viewing application as merely one element of your sermon or a list of to-dos at the end. You want to weave application into your entire message. You should always be communicating how your points apply to a variety of different life situations and circumstances. You want your teaching and application to become seamlessly woven together so that your listeners naturally follow you from propositional truth to illustration to application and back without realizing they ever left.

Think back to the original problem you presented at the beginning of the sermon. You began by making sure everyone in the room *felt* the problem. When presenting possible applications describe how your listeners can *apply* the solution to the problem. You are moving them from feeling the problem to solving the problem.

Put simply, application is when your listeners live out the truths you teach from Scripture. Your job as a communicator is to make sure your listeners are clear about what it looks like to live out what you are teaching.

BREAKING OUT OF WRITER'S BLOCK

Finally, even when you know all the best practices for developing your outlines, illustrations, and applications, sometimes you will find that you cannot break through a clogged mind and put pen to paper (or words on the screen). This is a sermon-prep rut, and there is a way out.

Sometimes my sermon comes together like a beautifully crafted work of art. Other times I struggle to make progress in my study. It is hard to break out of sermon prep stuck-ness. I have learned a few things that help me overcome these stuck times and want to share them with you. Here are 15 things you can do this week to get unstuck in your sermon prep.

1. *Put away your study materials and pray for 10 minutes about nothing but your sermon.* Preaching is supernatural work, and prayer reemphasizes in your own heart that you are utterly dependent on God to empower you to preach effectively.
2. *Read the text five times slowly.* It is amazing how quickly we tend to move away from the text and begin to look at study materials and focus on sermon formulation. Put away everything else and just read the text multiples times and let it speak to you.
3. *Open the voice memo app on your smart phone, hit record, and start preaching what you have so far.* You may find that speaking the words helps you formulate them better or in a different way from writing.
4. *Run your content by someone else and see what he or she thinks.* You can do this informally with a friend or fellow pastor or your preaching team.
5. *Take a break from studying for a while and come back to it later.* If your mind is foggy, walk away from it for a while. Think about something else. Do completely unrelated work for a few hours.
6. *Go for a walk—a brisk walk—or a run.* Get your

blood pumping and some much needed oxygen to your brain.

7. *When any thought about your sermon comes to mind during the week immediately make a note of it.* Immediately. Never assume that you will remember the amazing insights that come to you at random times during the week.
8. *Summarize the entire message in one paragraph.* Wherever you are in your study, distill the whole message into one paragraph. This will force you to focus and clarify what you are trying to communicate.
9. *Talk about your content with anyone who will talk about it with you.* Listen and take notes. This is similar to number 4, but the difference is that you do more listening than presenting. Fish the idea out just enough to get them to comment on it and then listen carefully and take notes.
10. *Do something kind for another human being.* It is amazing how serving someone can get you out of a rut.
11. *Scroll your Facebook NewsFeed and read the first three articles your friends posted.* Think through how you could use them as supporting material or illustrations. Even if you do not end up using them, this exercise gets you thinking.
12. *Ask a question on social media about something that re-*

lates to your sermon. This is a great way to get input from a lot of people very quickly.
13. *Explain your main point(s) to a child and ask him or her if they understand.* The process of making your message understandable to a child helps to simplify it in your own mind. If you cannot explain it to a child, you are not ready to explain it to anyone.
14. *Summarize the entire message in one sentence.* This is similar to number 8 but goes one step further. This summary sentence usually ends up becoming my bottom line.
15. *Listen to a sermon on the same text.* Listen to how some other preachers have dealt with the text or topic you are studying. If you end up using their ideas always be sure to give proper credit.

LANE SEBRING

CHAPTER SIX

Who Do You Think You're Talking To?
Know Your Listeners Inside and Out

Not long after we were married, my wife told me I was using "preacher voice" with her and she really wished we would just have a normal conversation. I asked her what she meant by "preacher voice." She told me that when I start talking I sometimes default into giving a mini-sermon about the topic. I use a slightly louder voice and get kind of preachy. We had a good laugh about it, but it made me think about how that comes across to others.

She also told me that it is hard to interject because I go on and on without stopping. Her theory is that because I teach and preach a lot, I have trained myself to talk continuously without pause.

Although this "skill" is useful in preaching, it can be detrimental to your interpersonal relationships. One-sided conversations are no fun—in fact, they are not really conversations but monologues. Not only that, but if all you do is talk and never listen to others, your actual sermons become void of the meaningful depth you get from interacting with humanity.

Talking comes easily to me and listening does not. This is probably common for a lot of us who preach. If we are not careful we can become people who are always telling. Always sharing our ideas. Always jumping at a moment to teach an insight to a willing audience—even if it is an audience of one person and that person is not that willing. We can become this kind of person at the expense of becoming listeners.

Becoming a good listener is essential to becoming an effective communicator. When you get up to preach you should have a wealth of information running through your mind that you have picked up from conversations with other human beings.

Reading or listening to podcasts cannot replace this interaction. The kind of listening I am talking about is much more relational. It is the kind that allows you to have your finger on the pulse of where your people are and what they need.

If listening does not come naturally to you, as it

doesn't to me, what can you do about it? I have to work very hard to be a good listener, and I am still trying to improve. There are three things I do to improve my listening, however, both in my marriage and in every interaction I have.

Ask more questions. Asking questions is a great way to learn, to grow, and to increase your knowledge of the world. The best leaders have inquisitive minds—they want to know more. They want to know why things are the way they are, how they could be different, and what they can do about it. They ask questions. I have found that when I speak with another person, by simply asking questions I can begin to see the world through another's lens. This is one of the best ways to grow and learn. A conversation is a great opportunity to see into the life of someone else. To gain insight. To empathize.

I have found that asking questions helps put me fully in the conversation rather than letting my mind drift to other things. Asking meaningful questions requires me to listen in the first place. I have to be engaged in order to pose any kind of question.

Intentionally pause long enough for someone else to interject. I make a point of just shutting up long enough to invite interaction. I do this to treat my affliction of talking too much. I have to be intentional about pausing and inviting feedback. I sometimes ask, "What do you think?" and I actually wait for a response.

Have you ever been with someone who asks you a question only to answer it for you before you have a chance to respond? It leaves you feeling as though he or she does not really care what you have to say. You probably don't want to do this to others. So pause and invite feedback.

Listen well enough to give meaningful feedback. Don't just wait until someone has finished saying what she is saying so you can say something better than what she just said. That's not a conversation—that's a tennis match.

When you are in a conversation with someone, be totally in the conversation. Make the other person feel as though he or she is the most important person in the world in that moment.

These three practices have helped not only my marriage but also my preaching. They have helped my marriage because my wife feels that we are having two-way conversations instead of monologues. They have helped my sermons because I feel more connected to my listeners. I learn and grow and it helps me communicate better.

The best preachers are great listeners. Begin making these three practices a regular part of your daily conversations. You will be glad you did—and so will the people you talk with.

Your preaching will improve as you demonstrate that you know the people you're ministering to. You've listened. You've heard. It will show.

SEEK MORE MEANINGFUL FEEDBACK

There are few things more vulnerable than preaching. If you do it right, it is a moment when you bare your soul for the world to see. So it makes sense that you will wonder what people think of your preaching. You want to know if your sermon worked. Did God use it to move people? Sometimes you just want someone to tell you that you did great so you don't feel quite so awful about your mediocre sermon (we've all been there).

Most of us walk away from a sermon we have preached with this resounding thought: *Validate me, tell me how great my sermon was because I need to feel worthy as a person!*

Categorically positive feedback is acceptable from your mom or your spouse. We all need someone cheering us on. But if you want to get better at anything, you have to pursue more meaningful feedback from others. You should seek feedback that actually makes a difference. You want the kind that tells you if your sermons are doing what they are supposed to do—making an impact.

Most people do not give this kind of feedback naturally. If your listeners are trying to say something nice about your preaching, they generally stick to one of three responses:

> *That was a great sermon!*
> *Enjoyed your sermon!*
> *Your sermon really spoke to me!*

None of these statements is really helpful. They

might make you feel good for a minute or two, but they do not do anything to help you improve.

The key bit of feedback you are looking for concerns *impact*. When someone gives you feedback, you want to know how your sermon impacted them. It could be something you said. It could be the way you said it. It could be how you set up a point. It could be your application of Scripture. It could be virtually anything you said or did. All that matters is how it impacted them. This is important for you to know because it helps you understand how you are coming across to your listeners.

Most negative feedback is rooted in miscommunication between what the preacher intended and how it was perceived. The better you understand how people are perceiving you, the better you can communicate what you intend to your audience.

You are looking for feedback that is as specific as possible so you can get a good grasp on what is actually making impact on people. To make it simple, try asking for clarification. Going back to my example of the top three responses:

- "That was a great sermon!" You ask: Why? What made it great *specifically?*
- "I really enjoyed your sermon!" You ask: What did you enjoy about it *in particular?* Why?
- "Your sermon really spoke to me!" You ask: *What part? How* did it speak to you?

If you can get them to give you even one point of specific feedback, then it will be far more beneficial for you than 100 vague "good job" comments.

It may be awkward to do this in every situation, but do it as often as you can. It will help you know what is working and what isn't. To get better, you need better feedback. Sometimes you have to ask for it.

Responding to negative feedback. Louie Giglio says sermon preparation is like labor and delivery. After pregnancy and labor you are committed to your sermon. Delivering it is hard work, but it is so worth it because your little sermon is precious to you. You cannot imagine a world without your sermon in it. So when someone says your sermon was bad it is really hurtful. Try walking up to a new mother and telling her that her baby is ugly. After you pick yourself up off the ground, you will think twice about saying something like that again.

Your sermon is your baby, and sometimes your baby *is* ugly.

You have to be careful not to take negative feedback personally because it can often help you improve. If your listeners do not think you can handle it, they will likely withhold the negative feedback. You need to give people permission to be honest with you about your sermon even when they have corrective comments.

Without coming across as defensive, ask for clarification in the same way you do with positive feedback. (If you get defensive you will shut people down and they will stop offering you constructive feedback.) Usually negative feedback is more specific than positive feedback, so clarifying questions may be much easier for them to answer.

- "That was a terrible sermon!" You ask: Why, what *exactly* made it terrible?
- "Your sermon made me wish I were dead!" You ask: What were the *top two or three things* about it that made you no longer want to live?
- "I have never heard a more terrible sermon than the one you just gave!" You say: I could tell you about some great preachers' sermons you could download!

Finally, when it comes to negative feedback you don't have to take a beating. If you just preached the sermon, you are coming off an adrenaline high and you are in no position to defend yourself. Set up a meeting, give them your email, or politely thank them and leave it at that. Going toe to toe with someone after you preach is usually not productive.

CHAPTER SEVEN

The Holy Spirit and Sermon Prep
How God Speaks to You in Your Prep

One of my jobs in college was to shoot and edit video. I learned very quickly that producing a great film took many hours of work. I would carefully examine each frame and meticulously clip, sharpen, adjust, and remove anything that took away from the finished product. It seemed to take forever to create a short video.

This process, however, is entirely necessary. It is what separates a great film from a bad one. We have all experienced a poorly edited film. One in which the audio is fuzzy, the picture has poor definition, the cuts are awkward and misplaced, and the frames drone on for too long. When we have to absorb all this sloppiness it makes it difficult to track with the story.

But think about the best movies and short films you have seen. When you watched these films you got lost in the story. As the viewer you were not thinking about edits and cuts. You were free to watch the film and appreciate its beauty. All of those edits were carefully made so you could sit back and enjoy.

Your sermons should be like a well-made film. Your listeners should not see the edits or cuts. They should simply feel as though they are on a continuous journey with you. This only happens when you have adequately prepared so all your toil, all your hard work, is transparent.

The best preachers, like the best filmmakers, make preaching look easy. The reason it looks easy when they are delivering the sermon is because of all the hard work that went into it behind the scenes.

Preaching is hard work! It is work that demands much from the preacher. It is a burden, and it is heavy. High cost, high reward. This is why I've used the first half of this book on the importance of preparation. The majority of the work a preacher does is to prepare the sermon so that it is ready to go.

Since I've emphasized this so much, I know it could seem to some that I don't appreciate the Holy Spirit's role in sermon preparation. But I fully know the importance of the Holy Spirit's guidance during the whole process of preparing and delivering the sermon. I've experienced it time and time again.

I believe that both relentless preparation and an absolute dependence on the Holy Spirit are not mutually exclusive. You can and should be both dependent on God and well-prepared for your sermon. This is why I want to end this section by discussing the importance of the Holy Spirit's role in sermon preparation.

I get interesting feedback on my blog (PreachingDonkey.com) when I write articles about sermon prep. Well-meaning people sometimes respond with misplaced piety. Their desire is to protect the purity of the process and not tarnish it with technique. They see preaching as this otherworldly exercise that the Holy Spirit superintends.

In their view, whenever a preacher makes an effort to improve his preaching, the work of the Holy Spirit is thwarted. I want to deal with some of these bits of feedback and explain why I believe they are misguided. Here are some comments I have received in response to my writing on sermon prep:

"No need for preaching technique. All that matters is prayer and Bible study always."

This argument seems almost saintly. All we pastors should do is pray and study the Bible. The purity and simplicity of this approach seems unassailable. I mean, how could you argue with prayer and Bible study? I have received this kind of feedback dozens of times.

If you preach without praying and studying the Bible, stop preaching. Prayer and Bible study are assumed practices for every preacher. Nothing in my writing suggests that prayer and Bible study are not needed. What I suggest is to add to prayer and Bible study by improving your communication skills, becoming a better presenter, sharpening your storytelling abilities, and doing many other things to become better at getting your message across. None of these are *in place of* prayer and Bible study but rather *in addition*.

"I see nothing from The Holy Spirit here."

Sometimes this argument is made this way: "The Holy Spirit only works in sermons where the preacher is not prepared." This is as if the Holy Spirit cannot work in your preparation. He can only work the moment you stand up and begin speaking.

I wholeheartedly reject this argument. I am convinced that God can speak to me just as well on Tuesday as he can on Sunday. He can (and does) give me insights for my sermon while I'm pouring over the passage days before the sermon or at the gym thinking it over on a treadmill. To limit the Holy Spirit's guidance to be only possible "in the moment" is to limit God's ability to speak to you. He can speak to you whenever and however he wants. He can speak through the mouth of a donkey to get his message across. In fact, he did one time. That's why I called my website *PreachingDonkey.com* which provides helpful tools to help preachers communicate better. If God can speak through a donkey, he can speak through you… and me.

There is no disconnect between the Holy Spirit's power and rigorous sermon preparation. I find that when I have worked hard and am well-prepared, I am the most open to God speaking to me in the moment. Because I am not distracted by the thought of *I'm not prepared for this*, I am open and free to hear from God in the moment.

Great preachers understand fully that the work they do is a work of God. They also understand their own responsibility to do all they can to bring their best to every sermon every time. Paul says it this way in Colossians 1:28-29: "Him we proclaim, warning everyone and teaching everyone with all wisdom, that we may present everyone mature in Christ. For this I toil, struggling with all his energy that he powerfully works within me."

So how does the Holy Spirit work in our sermon preparation? The Holy Spirit works best in us when we are best prepared. God works within us as we work in his strength. Paul says he "toils." Toil is hard work, but he does it in God's strength. God honors diligent labor in sermon preparation.

This is why I will continue to provide resources to

help preachers with sermon prep. This is why I won't settle for anything less than the best I can do every time I preach. This is why I hope you'll strive to do the best you can as well. Now we'll begin looking at killer sermon delivery in the next section.

PART THREE

KILLER DELIVERY

CHAPTER EIGHT

Give Them a Reason to Keep Listening
Why Your Listeners Must Feel it Before They Care About It

I remember the first pizza I ever made. I was a teenager and hungry for some tasty carbs smothered with sauce and pepperonis. *How hard could it be?* I thought. I found a box of pizza dough in my parent's cabinet and went to work. This was going to be the best pizza! I wanted it to be deep dish. I wanted it to have so many toppings that you couldn't pick it up with your hands. I envisioned an award-winning creation of yumminess. I put all the ingredients together in a way that mirrored what I had seen other pizzas look like and popped it in the oven.

And I waited patiently.

What came out of the oven 20 minutes later barely resembled food, much less a pizza. The dough was so thick that only the outer parts had "baked" (read *burnt to a crisp*) but the insides were still completely doughy. The toppings had all fallen off into the burners below causing a pepperoni-induced burning smell and smoke that triggered the smoke alarm. Thus, the creation I had so meticulously prepared was a complete bust.

My pizza, though thoughtfully prepared, did not deliver. It went nowhere but the trash. The only delivery that day was Dominos.

Similarly, we can prepare our sermons until we are blue in the face, but if we get up to preach and cannot deliver, it is all a bust. This section explores the many facets of delivering a killer sermon. Discover how to deliver a sermon that makes all that killer preparation worth the effort.

Ryan had come a long way. He developed a number of great practices for effective sermon preparation. But in his effort to write doctrinally-sound sermons, his messages were becoming "just the facts." They were true, accurate, biblical, and even reasonable. But they were also dry and boring. While his congregation mostly agreed with his sermons doctrinally, they did not do anything with them. Their lives were not impacted. His sermons, though sound, were altogether uninspiring.

Why? Ryan thought. He was working hard to outline and structure his sermons so they were focused and pointed. He was committed to making sure his people knew exactly what they needed to know—and *that* was part of the problem.

Although Ryan was getting across the information he thought his people needed to know, *they* were not convinced they needed to know it. He was not taking time to show people *why* his content mattered. He just wanted it to matter to them. He did what a lot of us who preach do: He assumed his listeners would automatically want to know what he had to say. He assumed they were ready to hear it. He assumed that if he just helped them know what to do, they would do it.

As a result, he focused on his content rather than on how his people would best receive it. In his thinking, his people came to church on most Sundays already eager to listen just because they showed up. When we are not careful, a lot of us will do this.

You, like I, have probably dealt with this. It is easy to focus on your content and not really consider whether your listeners are ready to hear it. You have been studying your material all week and are totally energized by it. It is all you have thought about for days. You are so excited to finally share all these life-changing thoughts that are bursting out of you.

But your listeners are not there yet. They walked into

church with everything on their minds except your sermon. They have nowhere near the same level of enthusiasm about your material as you have.

That's the way it works. You care. They probably do not.

So what can you do? One of the most basic theories of communication is Aristotle's ethos, pathos, logos. This theory suggests that the best public speaking has all three:

- *Ethos,* a credible speaker
- *Pathos,* a message that moves people emotionally
- *Logos,* a message that makes sense

In other words, your listeners are subconsciously requiring three things out of you if they are going to give you the right to speak to them:

You need to be trustworthy. (ethos)
You need to move my heart. (pathos)
You need to stimulate my mind. (logos)

If you deliver all three of those elements your listeners are much more likely to give you an ear. But the order in which you do them makes a difference.

Many preachers who manage to do all three do not get the order right. They often jump right into the logos, the arguments, the propositional truths, the "here's-what-you-need-to-do" content that all of us who have the gift of teaching love. They do this before they have sufficiently given their audience a reason to listen. These preachers think, *If I can just convince them with logic, then they'll be motivat-*

ed to action. This is why so many sermons are frontloaded with content and arguments and then have a list of possible applications tacked on at the end.

The problem is, most of your listeners need more than the facts up front. They need to be moved first at an emotional level. Only then, will they be engaged enough to hear the reason behind it. In the book, *Well Said!: Presentations and Conversations That Get Results*, Darlene Price explains how people are motivated to make decisions:

> "Even more vital to persuasion than Logos, says Aristotle, is Pathos, which includes the right-brain activities of emotions, images, stories, examples, empathy, humor, imagination, color, sounds, touch, and rapport.'
>
> "Tomes of studies show human beings typically make decisions based on emotions first (Pathos); then, we look for the facts and figures to justify it (Logos). Audience members do the same. With your words, actions, and visuals, seek first to inspire an emotion in them (joy, surprise, hope, excitement, love, empathy, vulnerability, sadness, fear, envy, guilt). Then, deliver the analysis to justify the emotion.'
>
> "An engaging, memorable, and persuasive presentation is balanced with both information and inspiration. 'It speaks to the head and the heart, leveraging both facts and feelings.' "

If your goal in preaching is life-change, then wouldn't it be better to put some of the pathos ahead of the logos? To get your audience to *feel* a problem before they *know* the solution? This is why I suggest an outline structure that puts the problem first, then points to the solution found in Scripture (discussed in chapter 5).

You must keep in mind that although you are totally convinced of your arguments and why they matter, your audience is not. Take the time to do the hard work of bringing your listeners to the point that they want to listen. Andy Stanley calls this "building tension," and it is what every good storyteller does. Killer storytellers and communicators capture your heart first, and then point you to the solution or resolution

Preaching this way allows God to be the hero of every story. God is the answer to the question, the healer of the pain, the hope for the hopeless situation.

OUR MISSING YOUNGER BROTHER

I want to demonstrate how this works in real life. My church was facing a problem of missing a generation. Like a lot of established churches, we lacked any significant number of young adults. We formed a team of young adults to pray, research other churches in the area and around the country, and seek God's will for our church to answer the question of what to do about this problem.

After months of meeting and considering options, the elders and pastors decided to move forward with the team's recommended solution, which was one of the biggest changes we had seen in a while at the church. I was tasked with presenting the vision to the church in a sermon.

I could have stood up and said, "We've met and decided to make a change. Here it is. Any questions?"

In other words, I could have merely presented the facts. While the information would have been accurate, it would not have been enough to capture anyone's heart. It would have merely informed their minds without giving their hearts a chance to believe in it.

Instead, I chose to walk through the story of the prodigal son in Luke 15. Just as the younger brother was missing in that story, so our younger brother was missing in our church. A whole generation of younger brothers and sisters was missing. Pointing to the heart of the father in the story, I said, "This church has the heart of the father, so we will run after our younger brother, this missing generation, and we will bring him home."

Then I explained how we were going to do it. And by the time I was explaining the *how*, everyone was bought into the *why*. This is because they were given an opportunity to *feel* the problem before they *knew* the solution.

As a result I had several parents with young adult

children follow up with me either immediately or by email to say, "We're in! Whatever we can do to help let us know!" And they did.

GIVE IT A TRY

Try this in your next sermon. Before you get to the answer, really set up the question. Before you get to the facts, truths, and arguments, get your listeners to understand why they should care. Why it matters. Put the *feel* before the *know*.

When you begin your sermons, present the problem in such a way that everyone in the room feels it at a core level. Ask the questions in such a way that all your listeners think to themselves, *"Yeah, I've wondered that before."* Only after you have given them a chance to wrestle with the issue at an emotional level can you begin to walk them through answering the question or solving the problem.

The answer is found in Scripture. In Jesus. In the gospel. This approach teaches people to go to God with their real-life problems. It also demonstrates how the Bible and your messages are relevant to their lives.

The reason so many people don't listen is because they do not think it will make a difference. They don't think it matters. Preaching to the heart first appeals to the sense of urgency and prepares people to receive the head-knowledge necessary to make the leap to application. For the logos to work, the pathos must come first.

With every sermon you prepare ask yourself, "What would make people care?" Then do the necessary work to create content that makes them care so they can actually do something with it.

When Ryan began applying this principle, he saw increased interest in his sermons. There were more noticeable "light bulb" and "aha" moments when he could tell his sermons were resonating with people on more than an intellectual level. His teaching was moving hearts and beginning to convince minds. More people were giving him feedback about what they had done as a result of his sermons and less about how earthshattering his insights were. This is a good thing, by the way. Like Ryan, you may love to hear comments such as, "Wow, that was so deep." While this can tickle our egos, it is far better to hear, "Let me tell you how God changed my life in this way as a result of your teaching."

Ryan found it tremendously rewarding to be able to move hearts and not just stimulate minds. His newfound love of appealing to the pathos relates to the next breakthrough for Ryan. That is where we will go next.

LANE SEBRING

CHAPTER NINE

The Balancing Act That Makes or Breaks Delivery
Find Your Rhythm Between Intensity and Relief

Our friend and fellow pastor Ryan has come a long way. He has developed some intentional habits that make it easier for him to connect with his audience on an emotional level and get them to see the need to apply what he is teaching. He hit a roadblock, however, when he started to prepare a series of messages on a subject he knew would be difficult for his people to hear. He knew there would potentially be much resistance and was not sure how he would navigate through it.

Have you ever been preparing a sermon and realized

it was not going to be received well? You just know there are parts of it people will naturally resist? Although this could be the case with parts of every sermon, it is more pronounced in certain ones.

What makes a sermon a sermon is that it gets people to see a better way. A good sermon makes people unsatisfied with the status quo. It makes them want to change their thinking, change their hearts, change their lives.

Simply stated, a sermon is a persuasive speech. By their very nature, sermons are designed to move people to make decisions they may not have considered otherwise.

Knowing that sermons can naturally make people uncomfortable with life did not make it any easier for Ryan, and it probably doesn't make it any easier for you. We know some truths are going to be hard to face, but we do not always know the best way to present them while meeting people where they are.

When you face opposition to something you say in a sermon you want to figure out how to deal with it in a way that does not dismiss people's feelings. You do not want to be insensitive. People do not respond well to being disrespected by a speaker—especially a preacher. Your listeners will not respond well to having their ideas dismissed as silly or irrelevant. This is why you have to be very intentional about addressing concerns people may have in a constructive way.

The most effective way is conversational preaching. Consider what you would do in a conversation. Treat your sermon as though you are having a conversation with every person in the room. Let that inform your ability to deal with opposition.

There are many different styles of preaching. You may actually go back and forth between two styles in the same sermon. Timothy Keller, in his book *Preaching: Communicating Faith in an Age of Skepticism*, identifies three main preaching styles that vary in intensity. Keller states that a preacher can move between two or more styles in a given sermon.

Thus, although I am not suggesting that conversational preaching is the only way to go, it is helpful when you are making arguments that you know people will be opposed to or that they will find difficult to believe or apply to their lives.

A few years ago I started getting two points of feedback very often about my sermons from people in my church:

>*You come across very personable when you preach.*
>*You seem very conversational.*

They often describe how my approach makes them feel. They say my sermons are disarming because they can relate to me as though I am a real person—not a disconnected preacher who doesn't understand the world they live in. Because I seem authentic, they say, they trust me and want to listen. I began to track what made my own and others' preaching seem conversational.

A great sermon is a conversation. You want to make each person feel as though you are having a conversation just with him or her as the only person in the room, as though you are sitting at a table discussing a problem she is facing, a concern she has, or a big decision she must make.

I began to think about what makes a preacher come across conversationally and why this approach works. What I found is that two principles apply for engaging people with sermons. First, your preaching should be a paradox of disarming and confronting. Second, you should understand the principle that when you give people an "out" they lean in closer.

DISARM AND CONFRONT

A sermon is a paradox between two opposing practices: disarming and confronting. To avoid unnecessarily offending your listeners and earn their ear, you need to disarm them. Disarming begins long before you get up to preach. People are disarmed when they have a pleasant experience in the parking lot where they have adequate signage and someone directing them where to go. People are disarmed when they are greeted with a smile and know where to check-in their kids. They are disarmed when the kids' ministry area looks clean and feels safe.

They are disarmed by an engaging, friendly environment in the lobby. They are disarmed with a cup of coffee (provided it is good coffee). They are disarmed when the music is inspiring and engaging.

By the time you get up to preach, chances are there has already been a lot of disarming. Though depending on how well your church makes first impressions, in some cases they may have been armed instead of disarmed.

In either case, if you are to be effective when you preach you first need to disarm your listeners. You need to demonstrate that you are not a monster. You need to show that you are trustworthy. That you are likable. This is ethos, and as we saw in chapter 8, it is one of the three building blocks of effective communication.

The first time a person listens to a speaker she is not actually listening to what is being said, at first. Rather, she is making decisions about whether she likes him or not. About whether she should keep listening. This happens fast.

Disarming people well in the initial stages of your sermon can in part give you a conversational edge. Although you can disarm in a number of ways, humor is probably the best way if you use it well. When people genuinely laugh it makes them feel good. It puts them at ease. It makes them relax. If I am laughing, I am not upset or angry. For a moment, I am happy. And so are your listeners.

Relating to your listeners in a personal way is another great way to disarm. That is why some of the best communicators tell a personal story or do a bit of bantering at the beginning of a message. If done well, it can break down barriers and put your listeners at ease. It doesn't have to relate entirely to the rest of your message. As long as it is relatable and engaging it can have a disarming effect.

Don't overdo it, however! A story that goes too long or doesn't relate at all to your content can be viewed as a time-waster. Don't frustrate people by wasting their time trying to be relatable. You can be relatable and disarm merely by greeting your audience before diving into your content.

Another way to disarm has to do with creating real-life interest in your content, which we saw in chapter 8 in our discussion of the importance of making people feel before they know.

Though important, disarming is a means to an end. You disarm so that you can confront. You want your listeners to confront their assumptions, behavior, attitudes, and ideas. In the end, life-change is the goal. So, if you are disarming people merely to disarm them, then you have missed it. You have to follow disarming with confrontation.

Disarming gives you permission to confront. Let's go

back to your listeners' overall experience at your church. When they are disarmed on every level—from the parking lot, to the kids' ministry, to the worship environment, to your preaching, they are ready to be confronted. Well, at least they are more open to confrontation than they would have been if they had not been disarmed.

Confrontation is a dirty word to some people. It conjures up a guy with a sign and a bullhorn yelling "turn or burn" at passersby.

That is not what I mean by confrontation. I am talking about the art of getting people to look at life differently. If, for a moment, you can bring people to a place where they have to wrestle with life as it is, the right kind of confrontation has occurred.

This is not to say we should be offensive for the sake of being offensive. The gospel is offensive on its own. The New Testament refers to it as a stumbling block. Inviting people to turn from their sins and put their faith in Jesus as their only hope is in itself confrontational. The best way to earn the right to be listened to when you confront is to have disarmed first.

GIVE THEM AN OUT

Andy Stanley in his book *Deep and Wide: Creating Churches Unchurched People Love to Attend* discusses the principle that *when you give people an out, they lean in closer*. Rather than demanding that people listen and obey what you are saying, he argues, give them permission not to. It may sound like this:

You may not believe this, and that's fine, but consider what would happen if you gave this a try.

You don't have to believe the Bible is true to read it. You read all kinds of things you don't believe are true (the news, etc.).

If you're not a follower of Christ, you don't have to do any of this, but what if you did?

This is an interesting phenomenon—that simply giving people permission not to listen to or apply what you are saying makes them listen more closely. This gives them the choice. They don't feel "preached at" or told what to do.

Andy Stanley says that rather than telling people what's wrong, we should inspire them to do what's right. As much as we might think it shouldn't be this way, most people are not motivated by being told what's wrong with them. In fact, the New Testament teaches that it is God's kindness that leads us to repentance (Romans 2:4). Not his law, but his grace.

In your preaching, you never want to be all law and no grace. You don't want to be all truth and no grace. You want to show people that the love and grace of Jesus is truly better than their human efforts.

You want to earn the right to confront people about their sin and call them to obedience to God's Word. You earn this right by taking a conversational approach: disarming, confronting, and giving them an out. There is one more thing you need to do to take a fully conversational approach. It is a three-step process to make sure you are doing this well.

A CONVERSATIONAL APPROACH

I use a three-step process in my preparation that helps me preach conversationally.

Step One: When you prepare, think about the obvious questions or objections that people will have about the point you are making. In every sermon you preach, you are going say things people find hard to believe and/or apply. It is vitally important that you anticipate and think through these objections before you get up to preach. The best way to do this is to prepare in a team and get input from a lot of different people about your content (as we saw in chapter 2 in our discussion of the team approach to sermon preparation).

I was preaching on a passage in 1 Corinthians 7 that says married couples should not deprive one another but have sex frequently. I knew there would be some married couples listening who were not having all that much sex for a variety of reasons. I anticipated that these couples would likely find the text annoying or offensive. They might find me annoying or offensive for bringing it up. This is something I needed to expect and be prepared to deal with.

Step Two: Anticipate how you would answer that question or objection. Think about how you would answer the objection if you were actually having a conversation with someone. You probably wouldn't dismiss their arguments as ridiculous and stupid.

Rather, you would try to see things from the other person's perspective. You would probably make it a point to affirm something about what he or she was feeling. An argument in a sermon should be no different. If you truly want people to listen to you, you have to show that you are listening to them. That you know what they are feeling and that it matters to you.

In my example above, I had to think about how I was going to address the awkward tension that people were inevitably going to feel about what I was teaching. I made a list of every possible response people might have to the text in 1 Corinthians. Then I thought about how I would respond to each one in a conversation. This led to the next step.

Step Three: In your sermon, bring it up and have the conversation in front of everyone. Given that preaching is a one-sided conversation, you have to present both sides of the argument. Your job as a preacher is to give your people a voice so they know you are listening to them. This is so important because if you seem disconnected in your own little world of sermon preaching, the average person will dismiss you and your arguments altogether.

So in my example of preaching from 1 Corinthians 7, I decided to "have the conversation in front of everyone." What was the conversation? Well, it was just to bring up the fact that lots of people quickly dismiss a passage like that instead of obeying it because they just wish it would go away. By bringing this up I was able to challenge people to rethink their tendency to ignore the passage because it made them so uncomfortable and to deal with their sexual dysfunction.

Most of my time was spent getting my church to see the importance of obeying a difficult passage like that rather than dismissing it. Then, of course, because of the sensitive nature of the topic, I discussed how some needed counseling, some needed intensive healing to take place, some needed to better understand their spouse, and others needed to repent of their selfishness, turn on some Marvin Gaye, and get it on.

I acknowledged that although it was not an easy fix, it was too important to ignore. Thus, I urged people to face their fears and deal with it, just as I would have if I were sitting across the table from a good friend.

I have found that when I simply state the obvious and "have the conversation," people engage better with the content because it seems more believable and real. Give these three steps a try next time you preach. You will be glad you did.

BALANCE INTENSITY AND RELIEF

For your sermons to be most effective you should have moments of great intensity balanced with moments of relief.

I saw an interview with Mel Gibson about producing the *Passion of the Christ*. He said the scenes of Jesus' crucifixion were so intense that he knew he had to "hold the viewer's hand through the movie." This is why the movie goes from scenes of intensity to scenes of relief. For instance, a scene in which Jesus is being flogged and beaten was followed by another scene that shows him with his mother as a young man building a chair.

Gibson could have written the movie so that it began intense and remained intense for the entire film all the way through to an intense ending. The problem with that approach is that viewers can only take so much. There must be a balance of intensity and relief.

This same principle applies to preaching. I once preached a sermon on how to change. The content was intense as it dealt with the fallen human condition. I talked about addiction, abuse, pain, hang-ups, hurts, and everything in between. The general feel of the sermon was intense. It was heavy. When I finished preaching the first of two services that day, I could not shake the feeling that the sermon needed some relief. It was too heavy and overwhelming in a way that was not productive.

I know what some of you are thinking, *Wait! Heavi-*

ness is good. Intensity is good. People need their toes stepped on! That's just the Holy Spirit working on them! I do not deny that some intensity is needed nor that God can use the heaviness to move people. And I understand the power of his Word to cut through hard hearts and break down barriers. But we are communicating with human beings who need to process the intensity.

If your preaching is all intensity all the time, then eventually all your words begin to sound the same. If every single word is vitally important, then no words are important. You will get the most out of your intensity when it is balanced with relief.

In his book *Preaching: The Art of Narrative Exposition*, Calvin Miller speaks to this concept:

> "Eugene Lowry in discussing his famous narrative 'loop' speaks of preachers intentionally letting up on the tension, and creating a moment of relief in the tension. Dramatic and passionate preaching may establish a tight bond between preacher and listener but it doesn't do much for the humanity and relationship that ought to characterize the best conversational style. Only when passion and relief are interchanged and juxtaposed does the sermon achieve its best rapport with the listeners. All scream and no cream is not good preaching. Nor is a namby-pamby, droning conversational style. The sermon, like life, must come at us in a variety of modes."

As with most things, balance is the key in preaching. Raising your voice when you preach is fine—unless you do it all the time. If a preacher yells every word eventually there is diminishing return. In the same way, IF I WERE TO WRITE IN ALL CAPS YOU WOULD EVENTUALLY BECOME EXHAUSTED BECAUSE IT FEELS LIKE I AM YELLING AT YOU! Eventually, you decide that because EVERY word is important, then effectively NO words are important.

So raise your voice, lower your voice. Speed up the pace, slow down the pace. Pause dramatically, keep on talking. Use humor, be intense. Just be sure to vary your approach.

Effective preaching takes into account the complexity of human emotion. It also takes into account the fact that people come in and out of paying attention to you. Save your moments of intensity for when you really need to drive your point home. Give your listeners relief, and they will respond better to your moments of intensity.

DEALING WITH CONTROVERSIAL ISSUES

As a preacher you should never shy away from tough topics. If the Bible addresses an issue, you should too. You want to help your people have a holistic view of how biblical truth intersects with every aspect of their lives. But the more controversial the topic, the more important it is to handle it with care.

As churches are undergoing more scrutiny and your motives as a preacher are called into question, you need to have a handle on how to approach tough issues.

In the last few years I have preached on topics such as what the Bible teaches about alcohol consumption, sex and sexual issues, marriage, and financial giving. Along the way, I have learned a few things about how to approach these types of sermons. Here are some tips for preaching on controversial issues.

Be authentic. It is important when dealing with a sensitive issue to show your listeners that you are human and understand the gravity of the issue. You don't want to appear like an academic, dispassionate drone who only drops in to comment and then flutters away to another land. You live in the real world, you have relationships with people who see the world differently from you (or you should), and you know that not everyone agrees. Be real about all of that. More importantly, be real about your own struggles with the issue. Maybe you have had a theological journey to get where you are. Let your listeners into that journey. Maybe you have struggled to understand why the Bible teaches what it does. Be honest about it. Your listeners, especially the skeptics in your audience, will appreciate your honesty.

Don't try to shock-jock. Some radio personalities have made a big name for themselves by being crass and using coarse humor and strong language. It helps in some niches to set the host apart from the others and give him or her a wider appeal.

Some preachers use sensitive topics as an opportunity to use crass language and coarse humor. Their intent is to capture attention and foster interest in the topic, but that is not necessary.

I heard a preacher delivering a sermon on the destructiveness of pornography. To open his message he asked if anyone, as a kid, had ever combed through the pages of *National Geographic* looking for naked people. While raising his hand and asking his listeners to do the same, he said, "They were sagging, dripping, drooping, dropping, but you were looking!"

It was admittedly funny. The way he said it, his delivery—it was all good comedy. But other than making people laugh, I don't know if it accomplished much else. It may have relieved the tension, but it very well could have offended just as many people as it helped. And those offended may have chosen not to listen to another word. Is that really worth it?

To be clear, the goal is *not* to avoid offending people. Some people need to be offended. Some people are comfortable and need to be made uncomfortable. But don't use up all your offense on inappropriate humor just to get a laugh.

If you are covering a sensitive topic, it probably engenders enough interest in itself. Depending on your listeners, you risk alienating people who may be offended and decide not to listen to you. My suggestion is to avoid being offensive for the purpose of shocking people. If you take a biblical approach to a sensitive cultural issue, it will be offensive on its own. Tell the truth, use humor to relieve the tension, but do not seek to capitalize on the opportunity for a moment of attention-getting.

Let's think about humor for a second. Why do you use humor in a sermon? To relieve the tension. There is a purpose behind humor. It allows people a moment to breathe out, to release, to relax in the midst of the intensity. When used effectively, humor helps you accomplish your objective to inform, inspire, motivate, and change the way people think about an important life issue. You do not want a moment of crass or inappropriate humor to compromise your effectiveness.

Demonstrate that you are being thoroughly biblical. If you are giving your opinion because the Bible does not explicitly address something, then say that's what you are doing. Otherwise, point to Scripture and not your own ideas about the topic. This helps remove *you* from the equation and puts the focus on the text itself. When people take exception to your arguments, you should always be able to point to Scripture as your source. If they disagree with you, then you need to be able to show them that their disagreement is with the text.

Understand the religious objections from within your church. Some topics have the potential of offending churched people more than non-churched people. I gave a sermon on what the Bible teaches about alcohol. I knew there would be some in my church who held views about alcohol that were based in tradition or preference, but not actually in what the Scriptures teach about the subject. I addressed these biases upfront and challenged them to think biblically even if it confronted their traditions or preferences about the subject.

Share your material with others while you prepare. Before you preach on a controversial issue, make sure you seek counsel from others. I am a firm believer in preparing sermons in teams, and I believe it is even more important when the subject matter is controversial. We examined the importance of gathering input before you preach in chapter 2 when we discussed the team approach to sermon preparation.

Be well-informed from a cultural perspective. The hotter the topic, the more your listeners will have a vast understanding of it. You need to be on top of where the issue stands at that exact moment. If your data and conclusions are three years behind (or even one year behind), it will make you look uninformed and harm your credibility (ethos) as a speaker. If your goal is to get your listeners to view the issue from a biblical perspective, you need to demonstrate that you understand it from a cultural perspective. Speak into the culture with an understanding of the world in which your listeners live.

Approach it with confidence. In these situations you never want to be rattled or overly nervous. If you hesitate and tip-toe around an issue, it will put your audience on edge and cause them to question how confidently you hold your position. It will also make them think twice about adopting the views themselves. This should matter to you if you want to change minds and influence hearts. I discuss how to be confident when you preach while avoiding a prideful attitude in the Conclusion.

Approach it with humility. In your confidence you never want to appear arrogant. Few people truly connect with a know-it-all preacher. Approach the topic with humility and respect those who disagree. Preaching is supernatural work. God has to move in the hearts of your people for life-change to occur.

Consider providing a forum for questions and answers. These issues always bring more questions. You want to show your listeners that you are not afraid of questions. You may not know the answer to every question people ask, but it is important to demonstrate that you care what's on their minds as they wrestle with these issues.

Pray. This is the most important step. Pray while you prepare, pray before you preach, pray while you are preaching if you can. Pray afterwards. Get others to pray for you. Be well-bathed in prayer. None of the above practices will do you much good without an active dependence upon God through prayer.

CHAPTER TEN

Be Totally Present When You Preach
Overcome Distractions, Preach Boldly

Nothing is more exhilarating than preaching! There is nothing like getting in front of a group of people, opening the Word of God, and pointing people to Jesus. I absolutely love it. But I still get nervous sometimes before I preach. Maybe you do, too. A few months ago I was standing next to my wife just before my sermon. She took my hand, which was freezing cold, leaned over and whispered, "Are you nervous? Your hand is freezing." I nodded, "Yep."

When I get up and start talking I am completely fine. God calms my nerves, puts me at ease, and gives me a confidence that can only come from him. Perhaps the pre-sermon nerves might be a way to keep me dependent upon his Spirit's power. I am always motivated to pray like crazy before every sermon. There are three things that make me nervous before I preach.

If I don't feel adequately prepared. If I didn't get to spend adequate time preparing to preach, I feel it before the sermon (and during). For me this is a spiritual issue: It is my duty to prepare well for every sermon I deliver. There is nothing spiritual about depending on the Holy Spirit to work through me when I have not prepared well. That's like praying for God to help you ace a test you didn't study for. Your failure to study does not mean God should bless your laziness.

If the subject matter is going to be difficult for me to preach and for them to hear. When I am going to preach a difficult text or topic, I feel it before the sermon. I have preached many sermons on controversial topics. I do not shy away from difficult passages or issues. If it needs to be addressed, I will address it (see chapter 9 for more on this). But the pre-sermon nerves tend to increase when I know I am about to get up and deal with a sensitive issue that I could easily mishandle and cause a big mess.

If I am too concerned about what they will think of me. Preachers want to be liked. Most people want to be liked. But the pastor profession tends to attract a disproportionate number of people-people. We like people, and we want people to like us. Preaching can become our chance to perform for people. We want to do well so our listeners will like us and want to hear more of us. One of our biggest fears is being perceived as boring, unengaging, irrelevant, or dull. So we feel this pressure, and it makes us nervous. When this particular nervousness is intense, we tend to preach from a place of pride or fear.

Maybe you can relate to these causes of pre-sermon nervousness. Perhaps you have others. I want to share some things I do to alleviate nervousness before I preach. Some of these are practical while others involve mindset changes. They all help.

OVERCOMING NERVES

Find a quiet place to review your notes. This is a must for me. Some Sundays I preach three services in a row, but before the first service I need five minutes alone to collect my thoughts and read back through my notes. I have a systematic preparation schedule throughout the week that I described in chapter 3. But on Sunday morning, within an hour of preaching the sermon, I always find it reassuring to look back over the notes just to have one last refresher.

Think about your opening words and practice saying them. I am a firm believer in rehearsing my sermons out loud. I use the voice memo app on my phone to record my sermons on Thursdays for time and content. When I practice *how* I am going to say *what* I am going to say, it makes a huge difference. Knowing exactly what is going to come out of your mouth right when you step up to speak is a great way to banish some of the nerves. Practice saying your opening lines. This will reduce the uncertainty and calm your nerves.

Think less about yourself and more about your listeners. You are not the point. When you are nervous about what people are going to think of you, it is a good indication that you are thinking too much about ... *you*. Your sermon is for the benefit of the hearer, not the advancement of your ego. I have benefited from quoting this verse to myself: *For am I now seeking the approval of man, or of God? Or am I trying to please man? If I were still trying to please man, I would not be a servant of Christ (Galatians 1:10).*

Do not perform for people; serve them. The goal of performing is your recognition. The goal of serving people is God's glory and the good of the people. Keep your focus on serving your listeners and bringing glory to God.

Channel your nervous energy into passion for your content. Nothing is more contagious than passion, and your listeners desperately want to be inspired. Begin to see your nervousness as a gift because it is extra energy to expend during your sermon. Channel it into passion and preach with boldness and energy.

Pray like crazy. My favorite part of nervousness is that it always prompts me to pray. I feel so close to God in those moments before I preach because I feel utterly dependent on his power. I pray for him to do what only he can do—take my flawed, imperfect efforts and change lives by his power.

MANAGING DISTRACTIONS

Many things will distract you while you preach. Distractions can easily interrupt your flow, make you lose your train of thought, and potentially derail your message. It is important to prepare for potential distractions ahead of time. All preaching distractions fall into one of two categories: internal or external.

Internal Distractions. These exist inside your head. Your mind goes a million miles an hour while you preach. You think about a lot of things in the moment:

- You cannot decide on what will be your next word.
- You wonder how your message is coming across.
- You are not sure if you have adequately made your point.
- You realize you are not actually living out what you are preaching.
- You think about the argument you had with your wife that morning.
- You are concerned someone might be thinking you are preaching about them.
- You realized you have talked yourself into a cor-

ner and are not sure how to get out.
- You wonder if everyone is bored.
- You are fairly confident that everyone is bored.
- You are bored.

All of this is going on in your head while words are coming out of your mouth. It makes it difficult to stay focused on your message. These internal distractions come at you from your own thoughts. No one knows they are happening except you. There is another type of distraction that is just as disruptive.

External Distractions. These distractions come from something other than you, and they are largely out of your control. That crying baby... That gentleman who is gathering his things and leaving during your message... That family that is coming in late... That woman with an insidious cough...

What can you do about distractions when you preach? Whether they are internal or external, is there a way to overcome distractions? While some distractions cannot be avoided, they can be managed. Here are some ways to manage preaching distractions.

Expect distractions, but do your best to eliminate them. You will face distractions so you should just expect them. But you may be able to do something about them. While you cannot remove every distraction, you *can* work to prevent them:

- If you are hearing from that same screaming baby every Sunday, you could consider making the nursing mother rooms better or highlighting how safe and clean your nursery is (provided it actually is safe and clean).
- If people are constantly getting up and leaving during the sermon, you could consider putting a bouncer at the door (not really, but ... maybe?).
- If you find your mind wandering to things you are worried about, try to clear your mind before you preach. Prayer is a great way to do this.

You should expect distractions, but you do not have to resign yourself to them. Work to eliminate the ones you have control over.

Be well-prepared. Knowing distractions will come your way makes it even more vitally important to prepare well (for instance, by following the guidelines we examined in earlier chapters). The better prepared you are for your sermon, the easier it will be to deal with distractions. If you are having to think about what you are going to say next, you will be weak against even minimal distractions.

Keep preaching through just about anything. When I was learning how to preach, we did an exercise in which four of us preached a sermon all at the same time. I had to preach my sermon while three other people were preaching theirs. It was a great way to learn how to push through distractions. Practice the skill of continuing to preach even when you are distracted. Learn to push it out of your mind and focus on what you are doing. This is a learned skill. Get creative and practice preaching through distractions.

Do not be so tied to your plan that you miss an opportunity. Some distractions are an opportunity to answer a question or address an issue. Some distractions can also be an opportunity for humor. Acknowledging a distraction can be a great way to relieve the tension and lighten the mood. It can be incredibly uncomfortable to carry on as if a disruptive thing is not happening when everyone in the room sees it and hears it. So while you should keep preaching through just about anything, there is a time and place to make mention of a distraction. You just have to use your judgment and go with your gut.

Do not ever come across as angry about a distraction. This will make everyone even more uncomfortable. As the communicator, you set the tone. If you are rattled and angry you will set everyone on edge. Keep your calm, use humor, and be light-hearted.

And a word to the wise: Leave babies alone! Telling a mom to make her baby stop crying is a sure way to make a lot of enemies in a hurry. If you're going to mention the great nursery you have don't do it in direct response to the baby in the moment.

Pray. Prayer works in these situations. Sometimes you

cannot get rid of the distraction. You just cannot get that thought out of your head. But the sermon must go on. Pray in the moment and ask God to work.

AVOID USING THROWAWAY WORDS

A distracted mind is not a good thing in a sermon. It can lead to using throwaway words.

Pauses are great. They can add emphasis and give more weight to your point. A well-placed pause is a powerful public speaking tool that you should know how to use. But the wonderful effect of a pause is destroyed by a terrible public speaking mistake preachers make—the audible pause. What is an audible pause?

Well, um, it's uh, um, I think it's uh... (Sorry, just had to do that).

An audible pause is when you fill in the gaps of your speech with throwaway words such as "um," "uh," "you know," and "like."

These throwaway words are a huge distraction, and you must deal with them if you are going to stand out as a public speaker. To audibly pause is natural. To stop audibly pausing is a lot of work, but it is what separates the preachers from the donkeys. Here is how to stop using throwaway words in sermons:

Rehearse your sermons out loud. This is a vital step to successful delivery. It amazes me how many preachers do not rehearse their sermons out loud before they deliver.

Rehearsing allows you to know exactly what to expect when you get up to preach. You don't want surprises; you want to have a grasp on every detail of your sermon. Rehearsing enables this and keeps you from guessing in the moment and filling in the gaps with audible pauses. The fewer the surprises, the less the chance you will nervously use audible pauses.

Prepare well. This is related to number one, but in addition to rehearsing you need to be completely prepared for your sermon. How? Through adequate study and preparation, a clear state of mind, and enough intellectual and emotional energy to push through.

Slow down. If you are in a hurry, you probably have too much content. You should be able to articulate your points without rushing around and audibly pausing all over everyone.

Consider using a manuscript for a time. Although I do not use a manuscript, one benefit of using them is that you have a precise and thorough guide for your sermon. If you have a hard time shaking the habit of audibly pausing, consider giving manuscripts a try—type out your sermon word for word and print it out.

Queue yourself up for your next thought. One common reason speakers use words such as "uh" and "um" is because you are trying to think of what's next. Your next story, your next thought, your next word. Prepare your sermon in such a way that you have built-in transitions that queue your mind for what's next. When I preach, I have internalized my transitional cues through careful preparation and rehearsing my delivery. This lets me I know exactly where I am headed with the sermon at any given time. I have also organized my notes so that I can look down at any point and have an immediate visual cue to let me know where I need to go next.

Watch your game film. Watch yourself preach on video and keep track of when you use audible pauses. Look for patterns and work on eliminating them. It may feel awkward or embarrassing, but if you are serious about getting better give it a try.

Enlist the help of a friend. Have a trusted friend make a list of every time you use filler words in a sermon. He or she might have some insight on why you do it and help you identify patterns that you are unable to see yourself. My wife has been incredibly helpful to me in this area.

Get a foam hand and have someone smack you in the face every time you do it. Self-imposed physical pain is always a great way to train yourself to kick a habit.

PREACHING MULTIPLE SERVICES

At the time of this writing, my church has three Sunday morning services. Preaching three times in a day can take a lot out of you. Here are some practices that help me preach at my best at every service.

The biggest challenge for me is maintaining and sustaining energy for all three services. I arrive at the church at 8:00 a.m. and hit the ground running with the first service beginning at 9:15 a.m. The second service is at 11:00 a.m. and the third is at 12:45 p.m. By the time the 12:45 service is over, I have been going hard all day—preaching, talking to people, and pouring myself out. It can be a long day. A great day, but a long one.

Preaching is such an energizing activity for me. I am sure it is for you, too. I will have these huge adrenaline highs while I am preaching, then I come off the high just in time to preach again, which brings me back up. I repeat this process for the next service, then I go home and collapse.

But the people at the second service shouldn't get any less energy and commitment than the people in the first service. And the people attending the third service deserve the best I can give them as well. In order to ensure that I am bringing my best to every sermon, I have developed practices and systems that keep me energized all day.

This is my 7-step survival guide for preaching multiple services. If you are going to successfully preach two or more services in a morning you need to prepare and plan for endurance. Here are some things that will help ensure your success. Some of these are painfully obvious, but those are often the ones we neglect.

Get a solid night's sleep. You want to wake up on Sunday feeling well rested and ready to take on the day. Because I wake up at 6:30, I make sure I am in bed by 10:30.

Eat a good breakfast. Food is so important on a day that you preach multiple times. You want to begin your day with a breakfast that fuels your body and gives you lasting energy. I typically make myself a three-egg omelet, oatmeal, and a grapefruit. This is a larger breakfast than I usually eat, but I do not want to deal with hunger pangs while I am preaching the first service. Some of you might be thinking, "How does he have time to make this breakfast on Sunday mornings?" I wake up early, and it only takes me about 10 minutes.

Drink coffee. If you usually drink coffee, don't forget to on Sunday morning! If your body needs a little caffeine to get going, give it what it wants. You don't want to be yawning during the first service.

Drink more water than coffee. Don't drink too much coffee. You do not want to be jittery. I just make sure that I drink enough water to offset the coffee a bit and make sure I am well hydrated and my throat is not dry.

Go to the bathroom between services (just after one and just before the next). With all of this drinking, you will need to use the bathroom. Few things are worse than having to pee like crazy right when you are about to get up and preach. Go to the bathroom twice between services if you can.

Eat a snack between services. This is *so* important! Your breakfast will not get you through to the afternoon. You want to eat a quick snack between each service. I have a routine that fits in a snack time. After the service ends I am available down front for anyone who wants to talk or pray with me. When I finish these conversations I head backstage for a quick snack. I grab a banana and a granola bar or mixed nuts that I stashed in a cabinet when I got there that morning. I scarf down the food, make sure there is nothing in my teeth, and then head out to the foyer to hang out with people. It takes all of five minutes and it gives me the fuel I need to keep going.

Guard your conversations. People will want to talk with you, which is awesome! But you need to know your limits. If you preach a message and have no time to go to the bathroom, sit down for a second, grab a quick snack, or even have a moment or two of silence it is going to be very difficult to jump into the next service with the needed amount of energy. Set a time when your post-sermon conversations need to be finished and have someone ready to take over if needs still need to be addressed.

CHAPTER ELEVEN

Deliver the Goods
Get to the Point, Nail the Ending

How you begin your sermon is vital. It can mean the difference between your listeners' either checking out or deciding to pay close attention. The things you say at the beginning of a sermon are what your listeners subconsciously use to build a framework for your whole message. If your thoughts are murky and unclear, you are laying an unstable foundation.

The first 90 seconds of your sermon are some of the most powerful seconds you have. Do not waste them. Your listeners decide within these first 90 seconds whether they will keep listening to you or not. This is particularly true if they do not know you. But even if they do know you and like you as a preacher, every Sunday is a new opportunity to engage them or lose them. And both engagement and disengagement happen faster than you think.

Given how important the first few minutes of the sermon are, here are 3 must-dos of a strong sermon opening:

Start high. When you step onto the stage to present the Word of God you should be thrilled! You should revel in the privilege you have to teach people about the love God has for them. And it should show. Smile. Greet your listeners. Be genuinely energetic and enthusiastic about your content. Your people don't show up with the same enthusiasm for your sermon that you have. It is your job to lead the way by example.

Chris Hodges at Church of the Highlands in Birmingham, AL, does this well. One of the best examples is a sermon he gave on financial generosity. He approached a touchy topic with enthusiasm and energy right off the bat. This made the topic more bearable for his listeners. Implicitly, your listeners are taking their cues on how to feel about your content from you. If you come out of the gate high with authentic excitement for what everyone is about to discover in God's Word, they will follow your lead.

Start clear. Starting high only gets you so far. If you are energetic but fuzzy, your listeners will discredit your enthusiasm as lacking substance. Let people know exactly where you are going and why it matters. And do this as soon as possible while not seeming rushed or robotic. See chapter 8 where we discussed building tension for guidelines on introduce a topic and fostering interest in it.

Start now. Time is of the essence because you need to capture people quickly. Avoid rambling and wasting time. Get to the point and get there soon.

Starting high, clear, and now will get you on the way to a great delivery. But a great opener can be nullified by a common mistake a lot of us preachers make: preaching too long.

SHORTER SERMONS ARE ALMOST ALWAYS BETTER

Here is a principle of preaching you can count on: *Shorter sermons are almost always better.* You might say, "Well, Matt Chandler, pastor of The Village Church in Dallas, TX, speaks for an hour and he has hundreds of thousands of people listening to him!" Okay, sure, but he is not the norm. He is an anomaly. Not everybody can do what Matt Chandler does. But even if you can do all of those things for an hour, it does not mean you should. Few public speakers can keep an audience's attention for that long. Few should even try. There are three important reasons why shorter sermons are almost always better:

You don't need to say everything in a single sermon. We often think back on a sermon and ask ourselves: Did I say all the words I needed to say? The better question is: Did they hear what they needed to hear so they can do something with it? Part of the reason you may speak for a long time is that you think you need to say everything...

- Everything you could possibly point out that is in a given passage.
- Everything a Greek or Hebrew word could mean.
- Everything you learned in your study.
- Everything that's on your mind that day.

If you are saying everything, then I can promise you that your audience is not hearing what they need to hear. Saying everything is a great way to ensure your listeners hear nothing.

You write a better sermon when you have a time-limit. It is much more difficult to write a sermon when there is a hard time-limit. But if you put in the work and stick to the limit, you will deliver a much better product.

If you have an open-ended, ramble-all-you-want kind of situation, you will probably take it. You are a preacher. Preachers like to talk. Preachers like to have people listen to them talk. Preachers like to listen to themselves talk. Given the opportunity to keep talking, most preachers will take it.

Your sermon has a much clearer focus when you know you have limited time. You can only say what is worthy of mention, only what serves your sermon. You have to make decisions, cut things, put things aside (possibly for the next sermon), and decide what is absolutely essential for the present sermon.

You kill what you said earlier by continuing to say what you are saying now. All that great stuff you said at the beginning of your sermon... You kill it at the end by continuing to ramble. Your listeners will not be able to remember anything you said at the beginning of your sermon. They are thinking about lunch. They see your mouth is still moving and you are still saying words, but they are not listening. They would not have this problem if you had only stopped talking 10 minutes earlier. They see this as your fault.

This may seem harsh but it is true: Your message is way too important to risk losing everyone because you cannot stop talking. You reach a point of diminishing returns where your audience has checked out and you are talking to an audience of one—*yourself*. What I am suggesting is to have the discipline to communicate your message and let it be. Then let the Holy Spirit do his work in the lives of your listeners.

These are the reasons I went from 35 minutes to a hard 30-minute time-limit. Though at times it has been a challenge to prepare for a shorter sermon and stick to it, the payoff is huge. You may choose a different time-limit. There is nothing magical about 30 minutes. That is just what works best for our church and our context. Whatever the case, you can give it a try. If you regularly preach an open-ended "range" of time, consider experimenting with a hard time-limit. Make it a personal challenge. For example, if you currently have 40-50 minutes allotted for your sermon, try sticking to a 40-minute time-limit for the next four weeks. See how it changes your preparation and delivery methods. I bet you will find that your sermons pack a tighter punch and you have more focus.

If you are going to do this, the most important aid is a countdown clock. I cannot emphasize this enough. It is not enough to look at a clock on the wall—that same clock you look at and ignore every week when you've run over and notice your own stomach growling. You need a clock that is set for your desired time and counts down. I have a monitor in front of the stage pointing up toward me. No one can see it but me. When I start my sermon it says 30:00. Then the countdown begins: 29:59, 29:58, 29:57… When it hits zero it starts blinking red and counting up. The countdown made all the difference to me. I almost never go over now that I have a countdown clock.

If you are not set up to run it through your main system, you can always use the countdown on your phone and discretely set it up in front of you as you begin.

SWEAT THE DETAILS

Now that your sermon kicked off to a great start and you are on a time-limit, it is time to pay close attention to the details. In fact, I would suggest sweating the details. So much is lost in sermon delivery because of small things most preachers don't give much thought to. I have put together an assortment of delivery details you need to think through. You may not handle each aspect the same way I do, which is good because every preacher is unique. But you need to think through each one of these and do what you do on purpose.

Use of notes. I approach notes as a necessary evil. If I could completely do away with them I would. Maybe one day I'll be able to, but for now I limit my notes to one page. They fit in my Bible and I only look at them when I'm reading Scripture or the rare occasion where I lose my place and need a trigger. For more information, refer to chapter 5 where I shared how I color-code sequences of headers and summaries in my notes.

No matter how you organize your notes, consider the potential distractions your notes could be causing. Do you flip through them to find your place? When you set them down do they take a lot of arranging? Each time you have to avert your attention to a logistical element such as your notes, you are providing an opportunity for your listeners to check out.

Tablet or laptop as notes. Are you flipping through

slides? Is the computer screen casting a light on your face? Does it look like you are making a boardroom presentation? If you use an electronic device, you should consider these questions.

Internalize every message. I do not have to look at my notes often because I internalize my message (as discussed in chapter 3). By internalizing I mean I basically memorize them but not word for-word. I memorize the sequencing of thought, the arguments, the illustrations, the opening, the closing, and the passage of Scripture. By internalizing in this way, I am not beholden to my notes and it frees me up to be more open to the Spirit in the moment because I am not worried about what my next thought is going to be. Because I am prepared I am free.

Record it ahead of time. As part of my preparation method I record my sermon into the voice memo app on my phone. This enables me to know exactly what the sermon is going to sound like when I deliver it. I can also check for time and make changes as necessary to get it in the 28-30 minute range I most prefer.

Reading from a manuscript? I do not use a manuscript and don't think I could make it work with my presentation style and personality. But I have seen some preachers do it well. If you use this method make sure to look up, a lot. You should read in a way that is engaging and break away from the script often enough to look at your listeners. Sam Storms at Bridgeway Church in Oklahoma City uses a manuscript and is one of the best in the country who preaches this way. If you use this method and want to improve, I would encourage you to check out Sam's preaching.

TV on stage. In addition to the big screens in our auditorium I have a TV on stage with me. The best way I can describe it is as a TV-on-a-stick because it is a large flat-screen TV on a movable cart that is secured by a pole anchored to the back of it. I got this idea from Andy Stanley who uses an onstage TV with every sermon. I like using a TV because it helps me better focus everyone on the content. Rather than pointing to a screen over my head or off to the side of the room, I point to specific words on the screen next to me. This is an effective way to draw people's attention back to my content. How does your presentation media draw your listeners into the content? It is important to be intentional about it.

Bible in hand? Everyone has different views on how to handle the usage and presentation of Scripture. I prefer to hold a Bible in my hand for the visual. I want people to make a mental note that I am not promoting my own ideas but teaching scriptural truth. The visible Bible may help some connect the dots. Additionally, the Bible holds my notes in place with a string so I just open my Bible to the middle and my notes (including all scripture references) are ready to go with no flipping around.

Simple slides. When it comes to slides, the simpler the

better. Aside from scripture verses and quotes, avoid putting several points on one slide. Consider a separate slide for each point. This helps your listeners focus better on the content you are speaking of in the moment rather than multiple points all at once.

Use of Table, Chair, Podiums. I use a tall table and chair rather than a pulpit. I find that the ability to sit down, especially when reading the passage, helps vary my presentation and make it more conversational. Not everyone is comfortable with the table-and-chair approach. If you use a podium, come out from behind it often. Or consider putting it off to the side and standing next to it. The more you can remove barriers between you and your audience, the better they will relate to you. And if you do use a table and chair, do not slouch. Sit up tall because if you slouch onstage it will look as though you are tired and dispassionate. You want to come across energetic whether sitting or standing.

Watch yourself on video. I cannot emphasize enough how important it is to evaluate yourself on video. Watch your game film and assess how gestures, habits, and speech patterns come across on video. As painful as it may be to watch yourself on video, it's important if you want to improve. You will discover some things you need to work on.

NAIL THE ENDING

The way you end a sermon is just as important as the way you begin it. If the closing of your message is unfocused and unclear, your listeners will walk away feeling the same way about your message—that it was unfocused and unclear.

When I first began preaching I would prepare relentlessly for the first five minutes of my sermon. I wanted my opening thoughts to be perfect. I would prepare the opening remarks and the body of the sermon with careful detail. But when it came to the end of my message, I would just let the sermon kind of close itself. I did not have a plan for ending my sermons most of the time.

The result was a lot of missed opportunities where I could have had a much sharper impact if I had called people to action or driven a point home. Instead, I just winged most of them. I have learned from these mistakes and now plan much better for closing my sermons. I want to share with you some of the mistakes I have made because a lot of preachers make them. Here are four common mistakes preachers make when ending a sermon:

Ending too abruptly. A sermon is a conversation. Even though you may be the only one talking, you are having a conversation with your people. As with any other conversation, a sermon conversation is better when it ends naturally.

In real life we give each other cues when a conversation is about to end. We do not just walk away when we feel the discussion is over. We make sure the other person knows the conversation is ending. We give him or her a chance to prepare for the conversation to finish.

When you preach, your listeners need to know the end is coming before it happens. You do not have to announce it with the old familiar "Finally, in closing…" Rather, you just need to give some cues that the sermon is coming to a close so your people are not caught off guard.

In his book *Communicating for a Change: Seven Keys to Irresistible Communication*, Andy Stanley discusses the effect on an audience when a sermon is ended too abruptly. He compares it with sitting in the passenger seat of a car and having the driver slam on the brakes. It is alarming and takes you off guard.

Giving no indication that your sermon is about to end and just saying "Let's pray" will feel like slamming on the brakes to your listeners. Take some time, breathe a little, and prepare your people for the ending.

Ending too slowly. On the other end of the spectrum is taking too long to close. A long, droning ending to a sermon can be just as bad as an abrupt one.

I had a pastor growing up who would say, "And one more thing as we close…" Fifteen minutes later… "And one more thing as we close." I couldn't trust him. It was frustrating.

A natural ending to a conversation does not go on forever. Give people an appropriate amount of time to know your sermon is ending, point their thoughts in the direction you want them to go, and end it in a timely way.

Continuing to ramble at the end of a message is one of the best ways to kill the effectiveness of your content.

Restating your whole sermon in summary form. Restating your points is fine. Restating the most important point is even better. But where most pastors go awry is when they use the last few minutes to say everything they have already said—just one more time. The old, "Tell 'em what you're gonna tell 'em, tell 'em, tell 'em what you told 'em."

This is not a good usage of your closing. You should use the body of your sermon to preach your sermon. Use the end to drive the point home, give the application, call to action, challenge, inspire, or encourage. Your ending is when you make your message stick.

Do not squander those valuable moments at the end of the message to say what you have already said in the same way you have already said it.

Failing to give a clear application or way to respond. One of the things that makes a sermon different from other mediums such as lectures or lessons is that a sermon is a call to action. To sermonize is to motivate people to change course, to live differently, to think differently, to do something.

One preacher, commenting on PreachingDonkey.com, had this to say about sermons that fail to give application: "I feel cheated if I listen to a sermon with no application. Information minus application equals education. Education is good. Education plus application is better. If there is no application it is a missed opportunity for change. Without change what's the point?"

You want your sermon to give people some handles to grab onto. The closing is a perfect opportunity to introduce or reinforce the application of your sermon. What do you want your people to do as a result of what they just heard? What do you want them to think? How should they respond? The closing of your sermon should make the answers to these questions crystal clear in every listener's mind.

WHATEVER YOU DO, BE INSPIRING

As I wrap up this section on delivery, I want to share a great area of passion I have: *that the local church would thrive*. I love the church. That is why so much of this book, while applicable to any form of public speaking and preaching, is mostly about preaching in the local church context.

My love for the church makes me want local churches to come alive with passion for what God has called them to do. As a preacher, you are part of how God leads people to action.

I recently met with a pastor who leads a thriving church in my area. He planted the church in 2003, and it has grown from three families to 2,500 people in attendance today. He spent an hour sharing a lot of fantastic insights about casting vision, setting direction, and bringing people along on a mission to reach the community. One thing he shared with me, however, struck me as perhaps the most valuable part of great sermon delivery in the local church context.

TELL YOUR CHURCH WHAT THEY ARE

"Tell your church what they are, and eventually they will become that." These words rang inside my head as he explained that his job as a pastor is to set the expectation high and let his church know he believes that is who they are. Eventually, they will become that.

Great leaders set high expectations and truly believe their church is capable of meeting them. This principle is the same in school teaching. If a teacher expects a lot out of a student, the student will likely rise to the occasion and deliver. If the teacher expects very little from a student, the student will meet the low expectation every time. Very few will rise above low expectations. People tend to live both up and down to expectations.

During our conversation this pastor told me a story from the early days of his church. It was Christmas Eve and they had one service in the elementary school where their church met weekly. They ran out of space and it was standing room only—wall-to-wall, packed with people. They were exceeding the fire-code, at full capacity. A few dozen people could not fit inside the building and were gathered outside in the cold winter weather.

At one point during the evening he went outside and realized the people bearing the cold were the regular attenders. They had given up their seats to let the guests have the good seats inside. He often tells his church this story and says, *"Let me tell you what you did. You gave up your seats so that people far from God could hear the truth of the gospel and follow Jesus! That's the kind of church you are!"*

He said that to this day being hospitable is part of their church's culture. When they run out of room (which happens often), the regulars give up their seats. His job is to remind them constantly who they are as a church. He gave a few examples:

- *You are the kind of church who gives up their seats so others can meet Christ.*
- *You are the most generous church in the world.*
- *You tell your friends about Jesus and invite them to church.*

Preaching is the best opportunity to tell your church what they are. Recently I gave a sermon on serving. At one point I said, *"You are a serving church! This is who we are as a church. We serve one another above ourselves."* I said it both because *I* believe it and because I want *them* to believe it.

Rather than saying, "You need to serve more" or

"This church doesn't serve enough," I would much rather point out where it is happening and invite others along.

Telling your church what they are invites and inspires people to be a part of the amazing work to which God has called them. It inspires them to become the hospitable, generous, serving people you see in them.

As you are working on all aspects of your delivery, never forget the importance of your role in inspiring your people to live for God. So often this is as simple as communicating to them you believe that is who they are.

LANE SEBRING

PART FOUR

KILLING YOURSELF

LANE SEBRING

CHAPTER TWELVE

The #1 Thing Most Preachers Neglect
How to Take Care of Yourself

The good people at Community Church loved Ryan because Ryan loved them. They knew it because he was continually giving and giving. He was available *all* the time. Literally, anytime anyone needed anything he was there. The problem was that, like all of us, Ryan realized he had given and given to the point that he had nothing left. He was drawing from a dry well.

Ryan was faced with the same thing you and I are faced with—the grind. The grind is when your ministry gets to the point that it demands so much of your energy that you cannot get your head above water long enough to tend to anything else. This affects your family and every relationship you have. It also affects your preaching.

I am not suggesting that you neglect the needs of your church. What I am suggesting is that you take time to work on yourself. On you, as a communicator. On you, as a preacher. On you, as a person. Because you matter. If you neglect yourself and your development, then it will eventually affect your church.

We all must realize that if we neglect ourselves, we will diminish. Ultimately, the benefit you bring to your church every week when you preach will diminish. But you can do something about it! You can adopt practices that keep you fresh, relevant, and growing.

You can stay on top of the gravitational pull that insists on your demise. In the sections below, we will look at some ways you can keep growing and increasing your effectiveness as a preacher.

LEARN TO LEARN INTENTIONALLY

What separates ordinary preachers from extraordinary communicators is a relentless desire to improve. This sounds so simple, but it is true: *The most effective preachers are continual learners.*

So many things are competing for your time that it is difficult to know which resources you should take advantage of. To help you with this, I want to share three things you can do right now to further develop your skills as a preacher.

Read great preaching resources. I once met with a young man who was in his sophomore year of college. He felt a strong calling to be a pastor and wanted to know if he should change his major and pursue ministry as a career. I offered him some books that would help him think through his decision. He declined them, saying, "I'm not much of a reader."

"Well, then you won't be much of a pastor," I responded without thinking much about it.

He was surprised at my assessment that he should either become a reader or do something besides preaching for a living. I feel very strongly that those of us who preach have a responsibility to stay on top of what is going on—to read, listen, and pay attention to what's happening around us. Some of the most important material you can read are resources that will coach you in your preaching.

There are so many great books on preaching. You can learn about sermon structure, sermon content, and how to properly exegete (draw the meaning out of) a text. Some of my favorite preaching books, however, will help you discover powerful ways to communicate effectively when you preach. Here are three you should have in your arsenal:

Communicating for a Change: Seven Keys to Irresistible Communication by Andy Stanley. This is a practical, insightful book on the science of communicating a message for the greatest possible impact. Andy Stanley's style and method of preaching have greatly influenced my own and thousands of other preachers'.

Preaching: Communicating Truth in an Age of Skepticism by Timothy Keller. This timely book does not disappoint. Tim Keller is a pastor in Manhattan and is keenly aware of the skepticism that the secular and secularized have towards matters of faith. This book will challenge you to think carefully about the claims you make, how you make them and whom you are making them to.

Preaching: The Art of Narrative Exposition by Calvin Miller. In this book, Calvin Miller challenges the reader to consider the vast impact of narrative and storytelling on our culture as well as on the biblical writings. God's gospel tells a story. So should your sermon. Miller will walk you through how to do it in this engaging, powerful work.

Listen to great preaching. This is the best time in history to learn from other preachers. You have free access to just about any preacher you want—and every sermon they have preached. The best preachers in the world are available to inspire you and help you grow.

Keep in mind that although you can *learn* from anyone, you can only *be* yourself. Listen to others preach and benefit from it, but do not try to be a duplicate. You cheat yourself and your listeners when you try to be someone else.

The key is to listen not just to hear a great sermon

but to figure out what makes the sermon work. What makes it *not* work? Why did it impact you? How did it impact you? Begin to identify things that great preachers and speakers do. Identify what characteristics you find common in great sermons. Experiment with them. See what you could adapt to your personality and make your own.

TAKE A DAY OFF, HAVE A REAL VACATION

Why are so many of us hesitant to take a day off? The truth is: *The world is not going to end if you take a day off.* This planet will keep turning if you go on a vacation. One of the best things you can do to stay fresh as a preacher is to take a break.

So many pastors get burned out and fatigued because they lack balance. They are giving 100% of themselves 100% of the time. This is not sustainable and will lead to an inevitable crash landing. The good news is that there are two simple things you can do to keep yourself from burnout: *Take a real day off and have a real vacation.* Why are these so important? Let me share a few reasons it is vital that you and I take a day off and have a real vacation:

God rested. God set a pattern of working six days and resting one. If your schedule is packed tighter than God's, and you think you have more to get done than he does, you need to loosen things up. God commanded his people to remember the Sabbath. To remember to rest. To recognize that God provides and even if you take a break from your work, he will keep providing.

It is a good example to your church. It is very common in most of our churches for people to work long hours with little work-life balance. Days off are hard to come by, and many people work non-stop. As a pastor you may be tempted to go along with this lifestyle because you do not want to be perceived as lazy. I don't either. I want people to know how hard I work. I want them to be aware of the hours I put in, the pressure I am under, the late nights and early mornings. The endless meetings, emails, phone calls and tough conversations. I want people to know about all I deal with. I am afraid that if I take a day off and people see it they might think I'm not committed.

This is a trap: the fear of others. Paul asked this important question: *"For am I now seeking the approval of man, or of God? Or am I trying to please man? If I were still trying to please man, I would not be a servant of Christ (Galatians 1:10).* Taking a real day off will help you overcome the need to please everyone and actually help you be a good and healthy example to your church.

Your family needs you. Taking a day off and doing vacations is a great way to demonstrate to your family that they matter to you. It demonstrates to them that they deserve more than your leftovers and are first in your life after God.

Andy Stanley often says, "Don't give up what is unique to you for something someone else will do"

(*Choosing to Cheat: Who Wins When Family and Work Collide?*). Someone else will eventually take your place as the youth pastor or teaching pastor or lead pastor at your church. But you are the only husband your wife has. You are the only mom or dad your kids will have. Do not neglect them for the church. Do not cheat on your wife with the church. Do not sell out your children for your ministry. The church is the bride of Christ; don't make her your mistress.

To avoid burnout and stay energized. You are only human. You need to refresh and refuel. If you are giving all of yourself all of the time, you will eventually have nothing left to give.

I want to share some of the things I do to protect my days off and my vacations. If your days off and vacations are truly going to be Sabbath rest for you, you must guard them and make the most of them. Here is how to ensure you get the most out of your days off and vacations.

Your day off must truly be a day **off.** For me this means that on Fridays I do not check work email, I do not work on church-related projects at home, and I do not have ministry-related meetings.

If someone asks me when I am available to meet I just mention any day besides Friday. I will meet someone at 4:00 a.m. on Thursdays for breakfast. I will meet someone at 10:30 p.m. on Tuesday night. But I will **not** meet on Fridays (with very few exceptions—and it would take a true emergency).

Saturday morning I jump back online and respond to email, work on projects, and have meetings. But taking Friday off gives me energy to get back to work on Saturday.

When you go on vacation, completely disconnect. Here is what I do: I totally delete my work email and calendar off my phone when the vacation starts. I do not take my work laptop. I make sure my email responders are on for voicemail and email. And I make sure that all my responsibilities at church are covered before I leave.

When I come back from vacation, I want to be energized and ready to go again. If the vacation only meant moving my work from my office to the beach, I would come back just as drained as when I left.

I used to think it showed dedication if I never stopped working. Working on vacation. Working on my day off. I thought these things would prove to others that I was committed and a hard worker. That is a terrible way to live. Working on your day off and all through vacation does *not* prove you are a hard worker. It just proves that you need more work-life balance.

I want to do ministry for a few more decades. A day off each week and uninterrupted vacations are part of what will help me last.

What does this have to do with preaching? *Everything.* If you are worn too thin from unrealistic demands on your time, you will not preach well because you will not prepare well. There is only so much of you to go around. Recharge.

NO ONE WANTS TO TALK ABOUT THIS

Many of us do not want to face difficult realities. I would rather binge-watch Netflix than figure this year's tax return. I would rather have some friends over for dinner than confront someone who has wronged me. I would rather start writing a new book than finish the five that I have already started. All of us have things we put off, things we avoid taking care of.

For me, my weight was something I neglected for a long time. I gained about 30 pounds of excess weight a few years ago. For some people excess weight is unavoidable for a variety of reasons. For me it was the result of sloppy eating and a non-existent workout plan. After getting married I got lazy and started letting myself go. I knew this was wrong, but it was hard to correct course after I had developed bad habits.

Here's the truth. You can wish it weren't true. You can be really upset about it. It can hurt your feelings. You can express how unfair this is, but ... your listeners make judgments about you based on your appearance.

A good friend of mine confronted me. "Lane," he said, "the world doesn't need any more fat preachers." He told me how, like it or not, people make decisions about whether they should listen to a preacher based on his appearance. I realized my effectiveness as a preacher was on the line because I had a sloppy, indulgent lifestyle and it showed.

Weight is not something we talk about very much. Even just saying the word "fat" makes a lot of people uncomfortable. For some it conjures up a lot of hurt and pain. My intent in this section is not to hurt your feelings. I only want to offer a perspective on something that I believe hinders the effectiveness of a lot of preachers.

You may be thinking of all the reasons I shouldn't be saying these things. You may be angry at me because it should not matter what a pastor looks like and people should just be more spiritual. You may be ready to quote 1 Samuel about how God looks not at the outward appearance but at the heart. And you may be surprised to know that I agree with you.

It *should not* matter what a pastor looks like. People *should* be more spiritual. And God does look at the heart and not at outward appearances. But I am not talking about how things *should* be. I am talking about how things *are*. God looks at the heart, but most of your audience is judging your outward appearance.

You can judge them for judging you, but that won't get you anywhere. I think a better approach would be to understand the importance of what excess weight can communicate. Especially if it is weight that you could lose if you were to put down the donuts and pick up a dumbbell.

If you are overweight it gives people an opportunity to dismiss what you say about certain things.

- Try preaching about the dangers of drinking too much when you eat too much.
- Try preaching about spiritual disciplines when you have no physical discipline.
- Try preaching about self-control when you continually overeat.

It does not work.

I grew up in super-conservative churches, and almost every pastor I had was more than a little overweight. They would rail against the "sins of the flesh" and talk about living lives that were set apart for God. In the same breath they would describe what they were having for lunch, which included large portions of fried, re-fried, and deep-fried foods. Nothing was ever steamed or grilled. Just fried. The result was a 350-pound man who was unwavering in his opposition to "worldliness" but strangely silent about health and wellness.

To me, this communicated a pronounced disconnect. Fitness isn't everything, but a complete lack of effort and total indulgence is far from helpful.

This is why I decided to do something about my weight. I lost 30 pounds and have kept it off for a few years now. It was not easy, but it has had a positive impact on my life and ministry.

I also wanted to stop dishonoring my wife. When she married me I was a fit guy. Overnight I turned into a fat guy. This was classic bait-and-switch, and I was guilty. Especially now that I am a dad, I want to be here for my daughters for many years to come and pass along healthy habits to them.

As important as it is to work on sermon preparation and delivery, we cannot neglect to take care of ourselves. We can only be effective when we're fully engaged, healthy and balanced in our life and ministry. Don't let the demands of ministry steal your effectiveness. Take care of yourself so you can take care of God's people.

CONCLUSION

Preach with Godfidence

I want to end this book with one of the most important principles to keep in mind about your preaching: *it's not about you.*

As preachers we must guard against pride. It is a trap that can destroy our effectiveness and our ministries. At the same time, though, we need confidence in order to boldly proclaim God's Word. A tension exists between pride and confidence.

Most of us would say that being confident in our abilities is generally good, whereas being prideful in ourselves is detrimental. We know that the Scriptures contain harsh warnings against pride. Although you can be a confident person without being prideful, it often seems as though it is a very fine line.

A character trait closely related to pride and confidence is fear. Fear can be a huge inhibitor. Most of us bounce back and forth between pride and fear. Sometimes we are prideful of our accomplishments and look for others to notice how awesome we are and validate us. Other times we are insecure in our abilities and fearful of what other people might think. We like confidence because it seems to be a good middle ground, but it is difficult to stay there as a way of life.

PRIDE....... CONFIDENCE....... FEAR

I preached my first sermon when I was 17. People praised me for my deep insights and how well I communicated them. But those "deep insights" weren't mine. I had stolen the content from someone else. I wanted to be impressive, and I didn't realize at the time that I was committing plagiarism. (I have long since stopped using other people's ideas without crediting them.)

At the time I was deeply insecure in my own abilities. I thought that if I actually wrote and delivered a sermon of my own, people wouldn't like it. I didn't think it would be powerful. My primary goal at that point was not to be used by God to change lives by communicating His Word, but rather to gain others' approval and validation. That was all I needed at that point.

My motivation was fear: "If I don't *wow* them, they

will overlook me."

In my own fear I also struggled with pride. "Look what I did! They loved it!" Both of these extremes left me feeling very insecure and lacking confidence. My fear led me to fake it, and my pride was based in someone else's work. That's a lonely place to be as a leader.

If pride and fear are two ends of the spectrum and confidence is somewhere in the middle, does that mean we should just be half prideful and half fearful? Surely confidence is better than that.

I heard Ed Young Jr., pastor of Fellowship Church in Dallas, TX, speak on this topic in a message to pastors. Talking about pride and fear, he said most of us lean toward one or the other. But instead of confidence being the safe middle ground, he changed it to *Godfidence*. Godfidence is different from confidence.

Confidence still relies on self. I still have to make sure that I am confident in what I am trying to do. But Godfidence suggests that my task is from God, my abilities are from God, and my gifts are from God. If I am Godfident, then I have a keen understanding of what God has called me to do. I understand it is not about whether I am fearful, prideful, or even confident. It is all about God and the task he has given me. If God has called me, then he has equipped me.

Godfidence seeks to give God all the glory. Those who are Godfident are not fearful of what others think or prideful in their accomplishments. They are totally bought in to the glory of God in all things—especially preaching.

I work hard to be as effective a communicator as possible. But I know this for sure: God changes lives, not me. God's Word, not *my* words, transforms minds. God's Spirit, not my ability to persuade, is what moves hearts. This is Godfidence.

I want to be Godfident. Not prideful in my abilities, nor fearful of what others might say or do. But Godfident in Him.

This is a form of repentance—a changing of mind. This book has focused on helping you communicate better by removing barriers to effective communication. You can work on and improve a lot of these barriers by tweaking your approach and technique. Pride and fear, however, are matters of the heart that no amount of coaching can overcome. You have to let Christ reign in your heart and mind every time you preach.

Every time you preach, pray something like this before you get up to speak: *God, give me a holy Godfidence in you today. Give me boldness to proclaim your truth.*

It is my sincere hope that this book has helped you discover some practical ways to improve as a preacher so you can more effectively communicate the timeless truth of the gospel of Christ to a world desperate to hear it. Preach on with Godfidence!

REFERENCES

Keller, Timothy (2015). *Preaching: Communicating Faith in an Age of Skepticism*. New York: Viking Press.

Miller, Calvin (2010). *Preaching: The Art of Narrative Exposition*. Grand Rapids: Baker Books.

Richards, Lawrence O., & Bredfeldt, Gary J. (1998). *Creative Bible Teaching*. Chicago: Moody Publishers.

Price, Darlene. (2012). *Well Said!: Presentations and Conversations That Get Results*. AMA Publishing.

Stanley, Andy (2003). *Choosing to Cheat: Who Wins When Family and Work Collide?* Sisters, OR: Multnomah Books.

Stanley, Andy (2012). *Deep and Wide: Creating Churches Unchurched People Love to Attend*. Grand Rapids: Zondervan.

Stanley, Andy, & Jones, Lane (2006). *Communicating for a Change: Seven Keys to Irresistible Communication*. Sisters, OR: Multnomah Books.

ABOUT THE AUTHOR

Lane Sebring is a pastor, speaker, and the creator of PreachingDonkey.com, a site dedicated to helping preachers communicate better. His articles have been featured by SermonCentral.com, Church Leaders.com, and Pastors.com. Lane has a B.A. in Communication and a Master of Arts in Pastoral Ministry. He lives in the Northern Virginia / DC area with his wife, Rachel, and their two daughters.

LANE SEBRING

LANE SEBRING

Printed in Germany
by Amazon Distribution
GmbH, Leipzig